Cúirt 21

The Cúirt Annual 2006

Alan Hayes, EDITOR

Maura Kennedy, COMMISSIONING EDITOR

ISBN 1–903631–82–3, paperback

Published by Arlen House for Cúirt on 11 April 2006

Arlen House,
PO Box 222, Galway
Phone/Fax: 086 8207617, Email: arlenhouse@gmail.com

Cúirt International Festival of Literature
Galway Arts Centre, Dominick Street, Galway
Phone: 091 565886, Fax: 091 568642, Email: info@galwayartscentre.ie

Cover image 'Kissing her Book' 2005 is courtesy of Pauline Bewick
Typesetting: Arlen House
Printed by ColourBooks, Baldoyle, Dublin 13

contents

5 ALAN HAYES / *Introduction*
7 EDNA O'BRIEN / *Writer's Block*
8 DUNYA MIKHAIL / *A Second Life*
10 MARY MADEC / *I am the woman who took the veil*
13 JAMES MARTYN / *Apnoea*
14 PETER SIRR / *Conversation*
16 JOHN F DEANE / *Call Me Beautiful*
18 LELAND BARDWELL / *Mother, Mer*
20 MARK DOTY / *Theory of Incompletion*
23 PATRICIA BURKE BROGAN / *An Teannaloch*
24 SEAMUS HEANEY / *Pangur Bán*
26 GARETH LYONS MCLOUGHLIN / *Martian Postcard*
28 BIDDY JENKINSON / *Ag Cur Sneachta*
29 LORNA SHAUGHNESSY / *Anahuac Dawn*
30 NIKKI GIOVANNI / *On A Rainy Autumn Day*
31 IMELDA MAGUIRE / *My country tastes of Blackberries and Brambles*
32 MICHAEL MASSEY / *Celluloid Sundays*
34 SHEILA PHELAN / *Cáit, A Fresh Snowfall*
35 EOGHAN NAUGHTON / *Showboat*
36 TADHG RUSSELL / *And That Was The Future*
37 ROBERT BLY / *Gravity*
38 CAOILINN HUGHES / *Split*
40 LISA STEPPE / *The Journey*
44 PEGGIE GALLAGHER / *A Bog Hole*
46 JESSIE FERGUSON / *Foodchain*
47 CAITLIN MAUDE / *Attack*
48 STEPHEN SHIELDS / *Useless*
49 FRANK COSTELLO / *Bombscare*
50 P D LYONS / *Waltzing Miss Jeanie*
52 LAURENCE O'DWYER / *The Potter of Luzern*

54 OLIVER MARTYN / *L'Amour/Love*
56 CHOMAN HARDI / *As clouds slide across the sky*
57 CIARON DAVIES / *Dead Heat*
60 PATRICK HEWITT / *Toulouse Lautrec at the Galway Market*
63 KEVIN HIGGINS / *Original Bohemian Writes To Ex-Boyfriend About Astronomy*
64 PAUL PERRY / *The Lady with the Coronet of Jasmine*
76 FIONA PLACE / *A Journey I Have Taken*
78 MARAM AL-MASSRI / *Every night the birds sleep in their solitude*
79 ABDELWAHAB MEDDEB / *Wandering*
81 EOIN COLFER / *A Fowl Tale*
88 TANYA FARRELLY / *Whiteout*
94 TERESA DAVEY / *The Hand of God*
99 MARY O'DONOGHUE / *Fowlers*
105 E.P. DE BÚRCA / *Vestigial Greece*
114 NUALA NÍ CHONCHÚIR / *Toys*
120 ZOE WICOMB / An Excerpt from *Playing in the Light*
128 ALAN MCMONAGLE / *Late Night Coffee Bar: 28th March 2004*
135 CRISTINA CONA / *The Devil's Daughter*
140 CLARE-LOUISE BENNETT / *Hand Me Down*
146 BARTY BEGLEY / *Hurling and Football*
154 MAGS TREANOR / *Framing the Past*
157 JOHN O'REGAN / *Moonshine*
165 DRAGO JANCAR / *Jump off the* Liburnia
173 LIONEL SHRIVER / An Excerpt from *Double Fault*
180 WILLY VLAUTIN / *Kid Collins*
192 CLARE AZZOPARDI / *The Green Line*
205 OLEH LYSHEHA /*The Mind and the Hand*
217 KEN BRUEN / *Priest*
225 RONAN BENNETT / Chapter one from *Zugzwang*
234 HUGO KELLY / *In Townsville*
241 ADRIAN FRAZIER / *'Where does spirit live?' Houses in Modern Irish Literature*
256 *Acknowledgements*

ALAN HAYES

Introduction: Small Town, Big Talent

In this 21st anniversary year of the Cúirt International Festival of Literature most will agree that it is one festival which has succeeded in getting its energy and keeping its feet amongst the creative people of Galway, seamlessly integrating local talent with the best international performers. And in so doing, it has clearly flown to great heights. These heights are seen by many. Galway is a small city that has more than its fair share of creative talents. The combination of a strong literary history in both languages, a vibrant bookseller presence for many years and large creative and academic pools has resulted in a melting pot of talent. From all this energy and interaction, many wonders have emerged. The dynamism and work of personalities from all of these 'worlds' has helped build an international record for Cúirt. And more importantly has helped nurture many of our talented writers. Cúirt, Galway Arts Centre and other organizations and individuals deserve our thanks for this.

This 21st birthday gives us a great opportunity to look at our local successes. Sales figures received from bookshops and from publishers reveal some quite startling figures. Some local writers are on the same commercial level as writers published by international publishing houses – and that is without the massive marketing and advertising budgets, powerful distribution networks and aggressive financial incentives that these publishers can offer. A random sample of some of Galway's best writers reveals major critical and commercial success, often to international levels. Included in this list must be Ken Bruen, Rita Ann Higgins, Mike McCormack, Mary O'Malley, Patricia Burke Brogan, Eva Bourke, Micheál Ó Conghaile, Nuala Ní Chonchúir, Joan McBreen, Moya Cannon, Dolores Stewart and Fred Johnston (Cúirt's founder). Galway also has a great pool of newer writers at earlier stages in their publishing career such as Gerry Hanberry, Órfhlaith Foyle, Tony O'Dwyer, Lorna Shaughnessy, James McGowan, Maureen Gallagher and Hugo Kelly. Most, if not all, of these writers have had a productive relationship with Cúirt at some stage or other, they have given to and benefited from the festival. Literary festivals are essential for writer development, and a welcome boost for publishers.

But back to this anthology which is a representative sample of unpublished work by key performers in the 2006 festival, alongside material originally published online in *West47*, Galway Arts Centre's literary magazine (which incidentally is always looking for new pieces from writers, for further details see www.galwayartscentre.ie/west47/notes.html – all work submitted is peer-reviewed anonymously). Also included in the anthology are pieces by some participants at Galway Arts Centre's creative writing workshops facilitated by Máire Holmes. As with all anthologies, the reader will find her/his own particular favourites from the pieces published here, and, hopefully, there will be many favourites. And for all those not able to go *cúirt*ing in Galway in April, this anthology will hopefully fill some of the gaps.

Discover the treasures between these pages – find new ways of looking at the world, uncover a new idea, or a novel way of expressing a thought or emotion. And smile.

We hope that your encounters with these words will be pleasurable. This makes the mission all the more worthwhile.

Editor, researcher, writer and publisher, Alan Hayes is an equality activist at NUI, Galway. His books include *The Years Flew By* (Arlen House, 2000), *The Irish Women's History Reader* (Routledge, 2001), *Irish Women's History* (Irish Academic Press, 2004), and *Women Emerging* (NUI, Galway, 2005), and he is currently working on a biography of the Gifford women, *"John Brennan" and Her Sisters* and a history of feminist publishing in Ireland.

Edna O'Brien

Writer's Block

Green braid
Hems the shore
Lilac, lavender and Prussian blue
Toss in the billows:
Until a downpour
Turns the whole world pewter
Water and sky –
No light
No words
The blank page

Edna O'Brien has remained amongst the finest contemporary Irish novelists since the publication of the controversial *The Country Girls* trilogy (1960–64). Other novels include *A Pagan Place* (1971) and *In the Forest* (2002); her non-fiction includes *Mother Ireland* and *James Joyce*. She has received many accolades including a *Los Angeles Times* Award in 1990 for her short story collection, *Lantern Slides*, and the European Literature Prize in 1995. In 2006 her new novel *The Light of Evening* (Weidenfeld & Nicholson) and two collections of critical essays, *Wild Colonial Girl* and *Edna O'Brien: New Critical Perspectives* are published.

Dunya Mikhail

A Second Life

Translated from Arabic by Khaled Mattawa

After this life,
we need a second
to apply what we learned
in the first.
We commit one error after another.
We need a second life
to contemplate it all.
We marry and divorce.
We need a second life
to find the right one.
We need time
to finish our prison sentences
and to go out and live free
in the second life.
Loaded with experience,
we need a second life
to understand all these things.
We need time
to learn a new language
and a second life
to practice it
and use it well.
We write poetry and move on.
We need a second life to know

what the critics thought of us.
Pain requires time
to dissipate.
We need a second life
to learn how to live
without it.

Dunya Mikhail was born in Iraq in 1965 and educated at Baghdad University. She worked as Literary Editor for the *Baghdad Observer*. Facing increasing harassment from the authorities for her writings, Mikhail left her native country in the 1990s, travelling first to Jordan and then to the US, where she studied Near Eastern Studies at Wayne State University. She speaks Aramaic and writes in Arabic and English. In 2001 she was awarded the UN Human Rights Award for Freedom of Writing. She has published four collections in Arabic, and one lyrical, multi-genre text, *The Diary of a Wave Outside the Sea*.

MARY MADEC

I am the woman who took the veil

Who in the year of our Lord
Nineteen forty two, at the age of sixteen
My mother weeping at the door
My father unable to say goodbye
Entered the Presentation Convent in Galway

Who made the best of hard times
A way to be educated through vows
Left the rudeness of country life for parlours
Haggards for manicured gardens
Who wept though for my mother's flowers at the south gable

Who tried to bring all at home
Up in the world
One rung at a time
Cajoling, advising, keeping in touch

Who could not know touch
Only the feel of a wimple
Gabardine, cotton, winter wool

Who was tortured by loneliness
Sacrificed, sacrificed
Could not go home
To bury a mother or friend

Had to wait for reports of how it all happened
Imagine all the scenes

Who worked by day at school
Who didn't like punishment
Believed in *mol an óige*
My mother's mantra in my ears

Who did the legion of Mary visitation
Emptied slops in Shantalla for the infirm
Like mother and father at home
Whom I could not visit
The rules said no

Who visited the home place
After Vatican II
The old kitchen strange and new
Echoing the absence of my father and mother
My brother and wife
Trying to understand how a cage of manners
Held tears back

Who had it hard
Measured pain all the same as something good
Suspected the soft life
Knew how easy it was to substitute
Self pity for love

Who looks to the young
To tell my story
Though I am a woman of my time
Tired now, ready to go
A lone survivor in my convent home

Who will persevere to the end
Believing that with the help of God
And his holy mother
It will all make sense

Who will leave no-one weeping
Over my tidy grave in the garden by the canal
Only a heron rising from the silence on a winter's day
A robin stopping to check the disturbed clay
Long shadows in the glasshouse
My cuttings lined up on the south wall

Mary Madec comes from Mayo but has lived most of her adult life in Galway. In the nineties, she studied for a PhD in linguistics at the University of Pennsylvania. Prior to this, she wrote an M.A. thesis on the Old English lyric. She now works for Villanova University in Ireland. She started writing seriously last year and has since been accepted for publication in *Crannóg* and *The SHOp*.

Once they blamed the gods,
but now it's called prevailing weather.
Conditions which in the night
lowered an opaque bowl about us all
and we awoke to a thick soup
just beyond the harbour wall,
so close we could stir it.
Except that no boats sailed,
yet all day engine sounds
prevail and sometimes a craft
will barely break the grey skin
before entering its tendrils
again. The locals shake their heads
and count the fishing boats tied up
and listen closely to the sounds.
'Apnoea' they say and point it out:
our whole world in a bowl,
all breath held as in a dive;
and we sophisticates lie in the oven heat
and breathe the heavy pearled air,
aliens, fighting back the nagging
fear, that all, maybe, is not as we suggest,
the opaque bowl, the ghost sounds and the rest.

James Martyn is a poet and short story writer. He lives in Galway.

PETER SIRR

Conversation

I put down the phone
and the years go by.
Twenty years later your voice
is unchanged, as if
as we paused to catch our breath
or press the receiver closer
our bodies lurched from us
and half our lives
fell through the conversation

or we go back and forth
and now as you speak again
I'm sitting on the floor
in an empty office in Merrion Square
clutching an antique phone.
Daily I abandon the typewriter
and the continuous paper
and leave the world on the table

to sneak a call through the crackle
as if we stood in ships in wind
and swayed: our two cities swaying
with small news. My copy's due
my roll of continuous paper
has rolled to the other side of the room

and now, much later, years later
now that the paper's gone
and the line shut down

somehow the conversation continues
somehow we lie in swaying water
and never alter, somehow the line holds
and the years stretch, snap back
and we fall out, come to, send
our signals out, always
finished, unfinished, always
plugged in to a ghostly exchange.

Peter Sirr was born in Waterford in 1960. He has published seven collections of poems with Gallery Press, most recently *Nonetheless and Selected Poems* (2004). *Selected Poems* was published in the US by Wake Forest University Press in 2005. Until 2003 he was Director of the Irish Writers' Centre and is currently editor of *Poetry Ireland Review* and Writer-in-Residence for Dun Laoghaire-Rathdown/Institute of Art, Technology and Design. He is married to the poet Enda Wyley and they live in Dublin.

JOHN F. DEANE

Call Me Beautiful

Broad-shouldered, big as a labouring man, Ruth
was egg-woman, slow and inarticulate,
flat-footed in her widowhood and her big sons

slap-witted, dun as she. I was ever dumb
before her, decades of harsh news
in the lines of her face, and a small smile

grateful for neighbourly busyness; each egg,
mucous-touched, she spat on and frotted clean
against black woollen skirts. Crucifix

over the door, painted Madonna on the sill,
her house was an island on chicken-shitted ground
with a harvesting of rushes, her world

not ordered by methodical thinking. Now I know
it is my own need disturbs me, to find
meaning and motive beyond the manifest

ungainliness, to seek the spirit's dance towards
divine friendship, and to vision her rapt
on her knees in a field of corn, gleaning.

John F. Deane was born on Achill Island in 1943. In 1979 he founded Poetry Ireland and *The Poetry Ireland Review*. His poetry collections include *Christ, with Urban Fox, Toccata and Fugue, New & Selected Poems* and his latest, *The Instruments of Art* (Carcanet, 2006) which has been shortlisted for the *Irish Times*/Poetry Now Award. In 2006 he will be awarded the Ireland Fund Bursary in the Princess Grace Library, Monaco and a collection of essays will be published, *In Dogged Loyalty: The Religion of Poetry, the Poetry of Religion* (Columba Press).

LELAND BARDWELL

Mother, Mer

(An Excerpt from *An Imaginary Sea Sequence)*

I am the keeper of the rocks,
I sit because its easier,
My body's tired
It leans towards the horizon
Where the storm
Lives with my mother
My mother lifts
And crashes at my feet.

I tell her
I am the keeper of the rocks
and linger here
To watch my mother recede
Gathering up these nestlings

My children huddle
In my mothers arms
As she humps and pulls
Them from me
I watch them go to my mother
Mother, I cry don't take them
But she crashes back at my feet

Dragging and crashing and dragging
I sit because it's easier
I am the keeper of the rocks.

Leland Bardwell was born in India in 1928 and grew up in Ireland. As a fiction writer she has published five novels, the most recent being *Mother to a Stranger* (2002). Since her first collection of poems, *The Mad Cyclist*, appeared in 1970, she has published four further collections, the latest being *The Noise of Masonry Settling* (Dedalus 2006). A co-editor of long-running literary magazine, *Cyphers*, Leland is a member of Aosdana and lives in Co. Sligo.

Mark Doty

Theory of Incompletion

I'm painting the apartment, elaborate project
involving edging doorways and bookcases,

two coats at least, and on the radio
– the cable opera station – something
I don't know, Handel's Semele,

and either it's the latex fumes or the music itself
but I seem never to have heard anything so radiant,

gorgeous rising tiers of it
at some point ceasing briefly,
then cascading again, as if baroque music

were a series of waterfalls pouring in the wrong direction, perpetually up and
up, twisting toward the empyrean.

When a tenor – is he playing
the role of a god, perhaps the god of art? –
calls for unbridled joy in an outburst

whose golden form matches the solar confidence
of its content, I involuntarily say, Ah!

I am so swept up by the splendor,

on my ladder, edging the trim
along the crown molding, up where

the fumes are concentrated. Is this what music is,
a seemingly endless chain of glorious conclusions?

I am stroking the paint onto
every formerly white inch,
and of course I know Semele will end,

but it doesn't seem it ever has to; this writhing
stacked superb filigree denies the need for closure

– let it open out endlessly,
let door after door be slid back
to reveal the next cadence,

the new phrasing, onward and on. I am stilled now,
atop my ladder, leaning back onto the rungs,

no longer painting at all.
I am the rapture of denied closure,
no need to go anywhere.

If God is entirety forming and reasserting itself,
then this is what the supreme must be like,

an endless, both the nothing
against which forms arise

and the variable patterns themselves:

self-enfolding, self-devouring of which Handel
constructs a model in music's intricate reapportionment

of minutes. And then there's barely
a beat of a pause before we move on to Haydn,
and I am nowhere near the end of my work.

Mark Doty was born in 1953 in Maryville, Tennessee. His first volume of poetry, *Turtle, Swan*, appeared in 1987. His third collection, *My Alexandria* (1993) received both the *Los Angeles Times* Book Prize and the National Book Critics Circle Award. Since then he has published *Atlantis* (1995), *Sweet Machine* (1998) and *Source* (2001), as well as the memoirs *Heaven's Coast* (1996) and *Firebird* (1999). His latest volume of poetry, *School of the Arts*, was published in 2005 by HarperCollins. He lives in Houston and in New York City.

A man shuffles into the gallery,
wellingtons squelching on polished floors.
Smell of fish follows him
as he moves among glazed artworks.
He stops and stares
at a painting of Loch Corrib.

He turns to a critic and asks,
'Ar chuala tú riamh and Teannaloch?
I've fished that lake for fifty years.
I've smothered myself in its heart-beat.
I've dived beneath its layered skins
and listened to its soul talk'.
The critic raises an eyebrow
and, glass in hand, walks away.

The painter, in designer-spattered overalls,
stands centre floor.
The man raises his voice,
'Ar chuala tú riamh an Teannaloch?'
Cameras whirr and flash
as painter and critic pose
for London photographers.

Patricia Burke Brogan is a poet, painter and dramatist living in Galway.

SEAMUS HEANEY

Pangur Bán

Translated from the anonymous ninth century Irish poem

Pangur Bán and I at work,
Adepts, equals, cat and clerk:
His whole instinct is to hunt,
  Mine to free the meaning pent.

More than loud acclaim, I love
Books, silence, thought, my alcove.
  Happy for me, Pangur Bán
  Child-plays round some mouse's den.

Truth to tell, just being here,
Housed alone, housed together,
  Adds up to its own reward:
  Concentration, stealthy art.

Next thing an unwary mouse
Bares his flank: Pangur pounces.
  Next thing lines that held and held
  Meaning back begin to yield.

All the while, his full round eye
Fixes on the wall, while I
  Fix my duller, weaker gaze
  On the paved, resistant page.

With his unsheathed, perfect nails
Pangur springs, exults and kills.
    When the longed-for, difficult
    Answers come, I too exult.

So it goes. To each his own.
No vying. No vexation.
    Taking pleasure, taking pains,
    Kindred spirits, veterans.

Day and night, soft purr, soft pad,
Pangur Bán has learned his trade.
    Day and night, my own hard work
    Solves the cruxes, makes a mark.

Seamus Heaney was born in 1939 in County Derry, Northern Ireland. He began to write in 1962 and has since held several academic posts, including professorships in Berkeley and Oxford, and is currently Ralph Waldo Emerson Poet-in-Residence at Harvard University. Regarded as one of the world's finest living poets, he was awarded the Nobel Prize for Literature in 1995. His immense body of work includes translations of *Beowulf* and Sophocles and his poetic works extend from *Death of a Naturalist* (1966) to *District and Circle* published in April 2006 by Faber & Faber.

GARETH LYONS MCLOUGHLIN

Martian Postcard

When the ball of fire hangs smouldering in the sky and glares down with menacing rays
Upon the long hairs of the earth
A beast with a thousand knives for teeth
Bounds along the grass
Guzzling and devouring everything it can find or see
Food is kept in tubes
And can only be opened
With the help of a metal star with handles.
Liquid falls from out of the air
And when the air becomes angry
It explodes and rips apart at the seams.
Sometimes
On special rituals
The sky will be lit with colourful explosions
And all of the tribes will come out
And gawp and whoop
With big green glass weapons
Firing them in all directions and drinking its liquid gunpowder.
Everyone is always happy when these rituals occur
Except for one country
It is always sad
A country two oceans away
Is throwing this party for it all the time
But still

All they do is cry.
This country is a peculiar one
With mushrooms growing as tall as to pass out the clouds
Growing with a quick burst
And then disappearing as fast as they came.
This is all monitored from a distance
With a black cube
But not for too long as it is usually substituted for something more
interesting.

After a short lived career in television as half of the horse in *Wanderly Wagon*, Gareth Lyons McLoughlin soon gave up the life of the sleazy poseur to go into writing. The transition went very smoothly and he now lives in Galway where he enjoys trying to catch planes at the airport. He is fifteen years old and is a pupil at Colaiste Einde, Salthill.

BIDDY JENKINSON

Ag Cur Sneachta

Thit sneachta mín
mín
ar an sceach
agus reoigh
ina néal bán
ar shneachta gorm
na maidine.

Chonaic mo shean-*lady*
'Po
Po-lar
Po-lar-bear ..'.
sa ghairdín
gur mharaíos é
le h-aon bhéim amháin dem scuab.

Ach mhair a chnámha dubha ar an léana
gur cheil an t-earrach iad.

Biddy Jenkinson came to life when a poem of hers was published in Innti 7 in 1982. Since then she has published several collections, her latest volume is *Oíche Bhealtaine*. A poet, according to Jenkinson, 'is a troublemaker by profession, one who looks under carpets, one who notices that the emperor is wearing designer clothes'.

Snow on Popotecepetl, the Sleeping Woman
yawns and stretches, a half-moon smiles crookedly
as the last lights go out in the valley and the parched
city licks the hillsides in search of moisture.

A blurred photograph falls from a wallet,
lovers seated on basalt columns an ocean away,
her arms bind his chest in a tight girdle
as though her life depended on it,
as though she could stop the wind
that whips their clothes and hair.

In eighty-five the gods thrashed in their graves,
the city shook, schools and hospitals crumbled;
only the infants in their incubators were spared.

Elsewhere their anger oozed and oozes still,
the slow-cooling fire that sculpted enigmatic causeways,
hexagonal puzzles where giants and lovers
pitch their wits against the elements.

Lorna Shaughnessy was born in Belfast and lives in Moycullen. Her poems have appeared in various literary journals and in *Song of the Forgotten Shulamite* (Lapwing Press 2005). Her translations of contemporary Mexican poets María Baranda, *If We Have Lost Our Oldest Tales*, and Pura Lopez Colome, *Mother Tongue*, are published by Arlen House in 2006.

NIKKI GIOVANNI

On A Rainy Autumn Day

On a rainy autumn day
I lay on sheets washed
In 20 Mule Team Borax
Hung to dry
By sun and southern wind
Smoothed
On to an overstuffed ticking
Mattress
Covered by a single weight
                    single stitched
                    quilt

My body drinks in
The cooling embrace
And I smile
Dreaming
Of my grandmother's laughter

Nikki Giovanni was born in Knoxville, Tennessee in 1943. From her first two collections, *Black Feeling, Black Talk* (1968) and *Black Judgement* (1969), to *Quilting the Black-Eyed Pea* (2002), Giovanni's work is elegant and commanding. Her honours include the Langston Hughes Award for Distinguished Contributions to Arts and Letters in 1996 and the NAACP Image Award for Literature in 1998, 2000 and 2003. She is currently Professor of English and Gloria D. Smith Professor of Black Studies at Virginia Tech.

Imelda Maguire

My country tastes of Blackberries and Brambles

My country tastes of Blackberries and Brambles,

of thorns and fallen leaves.
Her mouth is full of little apples, bitter sloes.
There is the must of autumn on her breath.

My country's coat is all pulled threads,
lost buttons. Her treasures have slipped
from torn pockets,
lost on leaf-littered paths,
among broken conker-shells,
beech-mast scatterings.

My country is no simple place.
Her heart has fool and fury written on it.
Her eyes range wide, settle seldom.
My country has an ancient, sometimes cruel face.

Imelda Maguire lives in Donegal and is a member of Errigal Writers and Glass Apple Writers. Her first collection, *Shout If You Want Me To Sing*, was published in 2004 by Summer Palace Press; she has read at a number of literary festivals, and took part in Poetry Ireland's Introductions series in 2002.

MICHAEL MASSEY

Celluloid Sundays

The End. Palms smack buttocks
as we pour through the open doors
of Fort Savoy, riding into a prairie
sunset, high in the saddle with the *Duke*.

We slow the horses through high
house canyon, pretending not to see
Indians on the rim. Cool hands hover
over Winchesters. At church gates
we silence their war-whoops.
Only good Injun's a dead Injun.

Horses pick their way down Clooney's
Incline, eat sweet grass in the lowland
by the river while we squint through
the smoke of contraband Woodbines
jawing wise and tough: *Man's best friend's*
his horse, dog's just Injun meat.

In the dusty street a mean wind spins
skeleton tumbleweed. *Man's gotta do*
what a man's gotta do. I twitch the black-clad
bad lad into the first move and before
his colt can clear his holster this town
is breathing clean air again.

Lanterns are being lit in houses all along
the street. I tie the trusty steed to the saloon's
hitching post and swagger in through
swing doors: *Where were you till now?*

Michael Massey lives in Kilkenny, where he is the co-ordinator of the Clogh Writers group and organiser of the Clogh Writers' Annual Poetry Competition. His poems have appeared in a variety of Irish journals, such as *Poetry Ireland Review*, *The SHOp*, *The Stinging Fly* and the *Black Mountain Review*. He has published two collections *The Hilltop Tea-house* (Rectory Press, Waterford) and *Nothing to Fear* (Lapwing Publications, Belfast).

SHEILA PHELAN

Cáit, A Fresh Snowfall

Took everyone by surprise
this morning, driving to work,
from Wicklow or the suburbs.
The morning after you were born
the landscape changed
to show each human footprint
or bird, or animal,
without grief or hate
barely grazing the earth.

Sheila Phelan completed an MA in Writing in the National University of Ireland, Galway in 2003 and received an Arts Council Bursary in 2002. Her poems have been published in a selection of literary journals, including *The SHOp*, *Fortnight*, *The Stinging Fly* and *Cyphers*.

Sometimes on Fridays after their civil service week,
they would take up in the good room with friends,
past closing time, red-faced from cold and drink.

Tony Rafferty had lost his shirt to the banks
but you would or wouldn't know it listening to him sing
Old Man River – as good as Paul Robeson in *Showboat.*

He don't plant taters
He don't plant cotton
An' dem dat plants 'em
Is soon forgotten

And then abruptly, he'd gather himself
into a bundle, face darkening,
exaggerated swaddling and sealing of coat,

dashing off to undercut any risk of display,
to underscore the vanity of show,
one broad hand pressing over his gut.

In the dark he'd fish out the bent spoon
and start up the Mercedes, the black boat
that was fast eating up petrol he could ill afford.

Eoghan Naughton lives in Galway. He has published in *Cúirt Journal* and *Poetry Ireland Review.*

Tadhg Russell

And That Was The Future

Once the sound we heard carried for miles
pulsing the breeze blown air,
plus its direction never varied.
A flat heavy sound
rumbling
inside a vault of empty space,
a weathervane message
crossing roads and fields
as we dodged
between the first big drops,
knowing for sure
that on a small island
a passing train, can only take you
so far.

Tadhg Russell lives in Doneraile, Co. Cork. He has been writing for the last four years and has had work published in *Cyphers*, *The Stinging Fly*, the Cork *Evening Echo* and a forthcoming piece in the winter issue of *Southword.*

ROBERT BLY

Gravity

Gravity lies close to the roots of laughter.
Both love the cabin open to the traveler,
The ocean apple wrapped in its own leaves.
How much joy that wrapped one has given us!
How can I be close to you if I'm not sad?
There's a joy in the madness that gathers up
Every last crumb of grief, and in the gravity
That makes the stone laugh down the mountain.

Robert Bly was born in Minnesota in 1926. He has published over a dozen highly-regarded volumes of poetry, beginning with *Silence in the Snowy Fields* in 1962. The best work of his long and varied translation career appeared recently in *The Winged Energy of Delight: Selected Translations* (2005). Bly's best-selling book-length essay, *From John: A Book about Men* sparked the men's movement of the early 1990s and defined a whole generation's view of masculinity. In his wide-ranging roles as ground-breaking poet, editor, translator, storyteller, and father of what he has called 'the expressive men's movement', Bly remains one of the most hotly debated American artists of the past half-century.

Caoilinn Hughes

Spilt

There was a language like Hebrew
going on at the next table,
tasting the energy of a first
kiss in every syllable,
bringing your tedium
like an audience into the house lights.
Your fingertips were dropping
tired drumming
on the metal café table
when you struck me –
the punch-line, onion-potent
and somehow permanent
in the faulty architecture of your face
though your eyes were almost traceless
as a runaway moon,
if it's not too much trouble imagining eyes
to be one thing, like a moon –
you always had trouble with detail.
From your confession onward
you were gone to me and I wondered
what I might have lost in the delay –
if the sun had fallen flat on its back
as wasted as an inside out petal
and I'd missed it,
listening to biscuits crumble.

I wondered if time had been and left
trails of tidy sky like jet lag
scudding toward the teasing surface
and whether it might have snowed,
whether all around outside
the landscape was laughing
hysterical roaring ranting rolling
chanting *I told you so –*
and what else you might have cost me
in the meantime.
Rough lips risked
forward pleading amnesty
for the first time I forgot you
facing me while patheticy
found its way into the dictionary
and let me use him in my calm fury.
And I am sorry now
I am so soft in my memories.
But I am still. Soft. Spilt.

Caoilinn Hughes is a student of English and Drama at Queen's University, Belfast. Her poetry has been published in many journals and anthologies throughout Ireland and the UK, including *The SHOp, Poetry Now, Crannóg, west47 online, Electric Acorn, The Lantern Review*, among others. Most recently she was published as part of Annir Publishing's *Anthology 1.*

Lisa Steppe

The Journey

The desert is beautiful, clean
and never lies. Theodore Monod

1

The plain was stupefied by heat.
A single tree, totem of dwarfish
animals, burnt emaciated. Memory
of winter solstice, our cool
shadows on snow. Or, think
of Lascaux, its narrow passageway
to the cave, that moment
of parturition before being born
into such fresh profundity. But
we are here, in the Algerian desert,
in the belly of sand, two lovebirds,
black insects, crawling.

2

We didn't know that, behind each
bush, eyes were wolfing us down,
spitting us out or stalking us for miles
on end. We had arrived where
dromedaries, ghostly shuttles on the horizon,

weave the poor man's tapestry:
a scab of red-rusted earth, blaring
billy goats, a blue stick
of a girl, dressed in ragdolls. At dusk,
pitching tent, invisible muggers
try to lay their hands on our
rucksacks, though our real riches
are mind-stuff, fool's gold: Hebridean
folk songs, Saxon charms,
Marvell's *and you shall see/*
I was but an inverted tree.

3

We follow mirages, talk
about Vester's *Die Grosse*
Vernetzung, the cosmic
web, rock nightly under
soaring constellations, say,
sun, sun-forests. Say, soul.
Do not see those ghoulish
figures waiting in ambush.

4

And again,
Camus's sun is sprung from the trap
of the night, clean, hard,
frostbitten. Soon after (why
not under cover of the dark)

the attack: rocks, that could kill
a lamb on the spot, are hurled –
not to kneecap but to kill. What
made you whirl round in time
to rip the rucksack off your back,
hold it up as a shield? Meanwhile
that magnificent silence of sand
and in the centre, on the deathbed
of our blue-eyed arrogance (taking
a benevolent world for granted),
our rattling breath. The previous
night, jackals were howling
by the tent. We nestled, listened
entranced, congratulated each
other for having tracked
down the 'authentic thing'.

5

Sunk in sandscape, whirlpooling;
tracks running berserk. Smoke.
Sac de cul. Dead-end. We take
to the mountains, slip across
the border into Tunisia, back
to business, to brown weasel-
boys selling souvenirs, the green
bones of Chalcopyrite,
Star Sapphire, Earthy Haematite,
Black Emery. Then the return
to civilised barbarity, traffic

lights, rip-off, our eyes
smarting of vastness. You
talk about 'navelwort', a rare
flower on cliffs. I talk
about cutting the rope.

Lisa Steppe lives in Dromahair, Co. Leitrim. Her first collection of poetry, *When the Wheathorses Die*, was published by Summer Palace Press and she has won many literary prizes, including the Dun Laoghaire International Poetry Competition, the Allingham and Boyle prizes for poetry and, for prose, the Listowel/Bryan MacMahon Prize. She has also been shortlisted for the Fish, Hennessy and Francis MacManus awards. Lisa Steppe has just completed her second collection of poetry.

PEGGIE GALLAGHER

A Bog Hole

hidden in heather,
she stumbled into once.

Dropped like a shot
through its gullet,

sucked in, chest high,
winter cold at her thighs.

Strong arms dragged her up,
The sucking mouth

closed behind her
with a slap.

He was like that.

Straddled across her,
he smiled, praised,

dazed her with wild promises
she half believed.

Then his body flailed
in a spasm of cold,

the hard set of his shoulders,
square hands

adjusting his cuffs,
the amber red in his eyes.

Peggie Gallagher is a poet and short story writer. She has been published in *Force 10*, *Peregrine 1999* (US), *THE SHOp* and *The Cúirt Annual* among others. She was shortlisted for the International Poetry Competition and awarded first prize in the Maria Edgeworth competition 2005 and is currently working towards her first collection.

Jesse Ferguson

Foodchain

chair and bed are tree and grass
in this complete ecosystem
in the dense weave of pillowcase
tiny bits of my skin
are chewed, in darkness savoured
by dust mites and other worshippers
microscopic pilgrims
subside in the warm
moisture of my morning eye
small paranoid things
lie awaiting my return to bed
are starving for manna from my scalp
here I am high priest, I the edible deity
and communion wafers flake off
my life-giving flesh
at the rate of one million per minute

Jesse Ferguson is a graduate student at the University of Ottawa. Raised in Cornwall, Ontario, he has been writing poetry for over six years. He is an associate member of The League of Canadian Poets, and his work has appeared in the University of Ottawa's magazines *Nexus, Innuendo* and *Yawp* as well as in Canadian, American and European publications, including *Ygdrasil, Stridemagazine, High Altitude Poetry, Spire* and *Zygote*. He is on the editorial board of the Ottawa literary journal *Bywords*, and is a consulting editor for *Quills Canadian Poetry Magazine*.

CAITLIN MAUDE

Attack

Translated from the Irish by Liam Cleary

Give me a hammer
or a hatchet
that I may batter and smash
this house
to smithereens
that I may make a threshold
of the lintel
and floors of the walls
so that the scraws, roof and chimneys
will come tumbling down
with the strength of my
sweat –

Hand me over now
the boards and nails
that I may build this other house –

But, Christ, I'm worn out.

Cáitlin Maude (1941–82) was born in Casla, Connemara. She was a renowned *sean-nós* singer, Irish language activist, actress and poet. *Cáitlín Maude: Dánta* was published posthumously by Coiscéim in 1984. **Liam Cleary**, born 1960, has published translations and poems in various journals and a collection of short stories for children.

STEPHEN SHIELDS

Useless

We've endured him now
for such a long time,
full frontal lobes like
the American fridge, albino
to its laminate and chrome
he easily dwarfs it.

He fits uncomfortably
wherever we put him,
trumpets in panic
as though the forest
were aflame, when
we should be asleep.

Sometimes he mocks me
from the shaving mirror.

The other thing: we dare not
return him to the king.

Stephen Shields was encouraged to return to writing after working as a lawyer when he joined the Athenry Writers' Group. He subsequently completed an MA in Writing at NUI Galway; he has been published in *Markings*, *Crannóg* and the anthologies *Turbulence: Corrib Voices* and *Maple Leaves*.

It was a blistering hot day as I sat in the back of the Mayor's car. The helicopter overhead hoovered in a scene out of a Vietnam movie. The year was 2015 and I was Mayor of Galway.

A Garda escort led out our car over the city's newest bridge to the racehorse. In the car I reflected on my life, the struggle with bi-polar and drink, and now, at 51 years of age, I was Galway's latest Labour mayor. My parents, I thought, would not have believed it, I was living out a dream, but this my feet were firmly on the ground.

As Michael my driver pulled into the futuristic Ballybrit Racehorse the crowds were overwhelming. Up to one hundred thousand people had gathered for the world's biggest day of racing. I was no racing fan, but that didn't bother me.

I met first with the President and then with the Taoiseach. However, I was not tempted to go into the Fianna Fail tent – the photographers would have had a field-day. Up the escalator, greeted by well-wishers, my life had come the full-circle. I wasn't getting carried away, and there was no room for complacency. The phone numbers in my mobile were all trusted friends, who all had gone through the struggle.

Sipping my orange juice, I settled back for the first race of the day. Everything appeared fine and on schedule, when just before the Galway Plate was due to start, I got a tip on my choulder from Supertendent Pat McGee. A phonecall had just been made to the racecourse. A bomb had been planted in one of the stands. What would we do?

Frank Costello took part in a creative writing workshop with Máire Holmes in Galway Arts Centre. He lives in Galway.

P.D. LYONS

Waltzing Miss Jeanie

The sky barely visible
Gunmetal cold keeps each bit of snow completely separate.
Sounds, most into silence or muffled by a swish and swirl
As my horse moves through.
Imagine sand against a giant hourglass,
Wicked witch of the west,
There's no place like home...
Nothing else moves,
Rock walls mostly covered
Drainage ditches camouflaged
Snow drifting levels the landscape almost beyond illusion.
By memory only we keep to the road.
Imagine being the first to cross this land in winter
And if it were a time before horses...?
Off the open ridge we cut down to where the pine woods
Shelter enough so we can pick up the pace.
Occasionally over burdened snow spills,
Sometimes peeling bits of green, chunks of old ice, thuds magnified by the quiet.
Perhaps an excuse to break the monotony
Or some primal memory aroused –
She spooks.
Imagine double barrel blast, a restless dragon, a living legend ...
So I talk her through; my voice being a calm place for her to focus.
So I sing, putting the name she knows into the song,
My father's curious choice for a lullaby he used to sing to me.

Imagine not yet five years old, frightened from things that you don't even have words for.
Things that move in those darker places in your room,
And then his heavy footsteps, the weight of his body as he sits on the edge of the bed, his strong steady
hands sometimes rubbing sometimes patting while always singing over and over until finally asleep
you couldn't ask him to again...
We make our way like that now,
Dealing with imagined as well as real risks –
Patches of ice beneath this rising snow upon this rising, winding road

P.D. Lyons recently returned from Canada with his wife and daughter to live in Fore, Co. Westmeath, where he works as a horsebreeder. His work has appeared in many literary magazines in the U.S. and Ireland and his collection of poetry, *Searches For Magic*, was published by Lapwing Press, Belfast.

LAURENCE O'DWYER

The Potter of Luzern

'Who eats the moon?' Katja asks.
'The wolf eats the moon', I say.

'And why does he eat the moon?'
'Because he is cold and hungry', I say.
'And why does no one else eat the moon?'

'Because no one else has teeth that are sharp
enough or claws that are long enough'.

'And does he eat the moon every night?' Katja asks.
'Yes, every night he eats the moon and he sleeps
on the hill when the sun comes up.

Every night it is the same trap; the moon rises and falls
till it is eaten away, and when at last it disappears

the wolf stumbles into town, dark with hunger —
that is when the new moon appears'.
'And who makes the new moon?' Katja asks.

'The potter makes the new moon', I say.
'He hurries down Dornachestrasse with it under

his arm and climbs to the top of Pilatus where
he lets it roll from his fingers until it rises
like a bubble in the eyes of the wolf'.

'And how long does it take to make the moon?' Katja asks.
'About a month', I say, 'give or take a day or two.

The potter must work from dawn until dusk, and every tavern
is closed to him; for if he drinks he will not finish
his moon and the wolf will come prowling

through the streets with his teeth and his claws'.
Late at night, we pass Herr Bacher hammering
on the door of the Machte bar. But they will not

let him in. We watch as he lowers his head
and turns for home down Einegasse strasse

muttering curses in the shadows
and shuddering every time he looks up
at the black sky.

Laurence O'Dwyer has published prose and poetry in magazines in Ireland and Britain. In 2005 he won a Hennessy/*Sunday Tribune* New Irish Writing Award for Best Emerging Poetry and was selected for the Poetry Ireland 'Introductions' series. He holds a PhD in paradigms of memory formation in the hippocampus from Trinity College, Dublin.

Oliver Martyn

L'Amour/Love

L'amour est plus haut les grate-ciels de l'Amérique
L'amour est plus vaste que l'océan Pacifique
Love is higher than the skyscrapers of America
Love is more vast than the Pacific Ocean

L'amour est plus doux que les chants sonores d'un oiseau
L'amour est comme le baptême où est lavé par l'Esprit et l'eau
Love is sweeter than the sonorous songs of a bird
Love is like baptism where one is washed by the Spirit and water

L'amour est plus beau que les fluers des tropiques
L'amour est une île où on trouve des trésors exotiques
Love is more beautiful than the tropical flowers
Love is an island where one finds exotic treasures

L'amour est plus grand que l'espoir et la foi
L'amour est comme Moïse qui donna á l'Israël la loi
Love is greater than hope and faith
Love is like Moses who gave to Israel the law

L'amour est plus paisible qu'un lac silencieuz
L'amour est comme Marie qui fut choisi pour être la mère de Jésus
Love is more peaceful than a silent lake
Love is like Mary who was chosen to be the mother of Jesus

L'amour est plus fort que les murs d'un grand château
L'amour est comme Dieu qui remarque la mort d'un petit oiseau
Love is more stronger than the walls of a great castle
Love is like God who notices the death of a little bird

L'amour est plus généreux que les douches d'avril
L'amour est comme des fluers qui poussent dans un désert stérile
Love is more generous than the April showers
Love is like flowers which grow in a barren desert

L'amour est comme Marie qui accepta la volonté de Dieu
L'amour est comme Jean, le plus aimé des disciples de Jésus
Love is like Mary who accepted the will of God
Love is like John, the most beloved of Jesus' disciples

L'amour est comme un enfant qui prie Dieu chaques nuit
L'amour est le soleil qui rayonne après la pluie
Love is like a child who prays to God each night
Love is like the sun, which shines forth after rain.

Oliver Martyn took part in a creative writing workshop with Máire Holmes in Galway Arts Centre. He lives in Galway.

She says, sometimes we glorify
a dead person, a short love affair.

Sometimes, she says,
we glorify a person because they are dead
we long for an affair because it was short.

Today is the day, she says,
there is no point in enduring the rain
while thinking of sunshine.
No point in thinking yesterday was fine
for this moment is.

But as the clouds slide across the sky
she thinks of him,
of the cold Christmas night
when she stayed awake
to watch him sleep.

There is no point, she says,
no point but.

Choman Hardi has lived in exile in the UK since being forced to leave Iraqi Kurdistan at fourteen. She has published three poetry collections in Kurdish and her first in English, *Life For Us* (Bloodaxe Books), appeared in 2004.

Ciaron Davies

Dead Heat

I

Old cowboy boots crumple down gravel
Long since dead with the red hot sun
Rusty Billy has got a gun
You can see it smoking
As he empties round after round
Into the hide of his favourite horse

II

All the old women come and go
The young kids too
Have found a wounded scorpion
And are doing just like Daddy told them
'Strike out first and don't even think
Blink an eyelid and you just got dead'

III

Here come those old cowboy boots again
You can hear silver spurs echo in the wind
And you can hear cold footsteps carry through the Dead Valley
A final gunshot rings through his old man's ears and twists his mind
He'd wipe away blood but its gone cold and sticky just like bad honey

In his head he can hear his long gone woman telling him what to do
The Sheriff too is crawling out of the woodwork with a warrant in his hand
The angry lynch mob have got a rope and the Scorpion kids are out for blood

IV

Delirium comes and our horseless hero finds himself swinging
The doors to the Last Chance Saloon violently open as he climbs inside
He screams to bartender Jake for service and punches the windows out
With a brick wrapped up in a broken plate of glass he got off a junky painter
And as he beats the horror into submission with a torn bottle of Bourbon
He can hear all the children and woman and lawmen laughing at him from
Beyond that place where every moment of the past mirrors the future
And all of yesterday's broken promises become tomorrow's newest mistakes

They roll with the dice and the blood drenched bottle fills shot after shot
Of thimble hope that takes us one step closer to the one way show down

V

Staggering out of the Last Chance Saloon with a gut-full of rot and a mind-full of hate
Rusty Billy felt the insanely hot sun beat down on his rubber-like and unshaven anaemic face
Covering his warn old eyes with his nicotine stained hands the horse shooting
old timer tried to
block out the sun

VI

It was the last mistake he ever made
Hiding behind the sun was a ghost of the past
From a killing long since done
And an injury long since festered
Revenge they say is a dish best served cold
Its worse then that
Its a goddamn disease
That won't ever stop
Until the frontier has built walls of bodies
Piled for miles and miles
As far as the Scorpion kids eyes can see
Its deathly testimony of yesterday's bullet
In tomorrow's gun

rip.

Ciaron Davies is a Galway-based poet, playwright and musician and is currently recording an album, *Too sick too sing,* which is due for release in spring 2006.

PATRICK HEWITT

Toulouse Lautrec at the Galway Market

I went early this morning to the market. After the rain of yesterday, the heat of the morning is causing the street air to be saturated with a hundred fragrances. I inhale them, trying to decipher their mysterious messages.

Some flowers, just a few, have transmuted themselves into beautiful women: a striking lupin dressed in bronze and azure blue is getting into her Audi A4, and a dark black-red tightly budded hollyhock is cycling away on her bicycle.

And on the main street, just away from the market, I notice a rare and exotic woman who has surely drifted in from Southern Spain or from North Africa. In fashion like that, she has spent the night in the luxury of the Radisson or the new Marriot Hotel!

Near me at the vegetable stall, dressed in cotton culottes, yes in black cotton culottes, and stocking-less in sandals, and wearing blue eye-liner, and a black top which is playing with the highlights of her blonde hair, is a thirty year old woman, choosing some limes with her long ring-less fingers.

Amid all the beauty and the fragrance and the saturation and the aroma and the heat and the colour and the air and the voices, she is silent and beautiful.

She moves through the crowd. I want her to ask me to run off with her to the nearest hotel. And there to eat with me, to talk to me, to torment me, to console me.

I know she must have perfect kidneys, and a urinary tract through which the sweetest aqua flows.

I, you will remember, have quite a fragile constitution.

I enter the cheese shop which is located near the market. A young woman sometimes serves me here. She has an aquiline nose, clinical glasses, black hair and an olive complexion. I am certain she is a Spanish nun from a convent in Toledo.

On my way home, in the empty car park, I detect the aroma of an interesting perfume. I find myself trying to detect its source, like a dog. But the car park is empty.

I cannot write without a bead of perspiration on my forehead. I miss living in a Mediterranean country. Instead, here in Galway, I make do by reading European newspapers. In Thursday's issue of *El Mundo* several pages express disappointment on the failure of Madrid to become the host city for the 2012 Olympics. There is a photograph of Arancha Sánchez-Vicario leaving the convention centre in Singapore, looking profoundly sad. She carries an open fan, with which she appears to be trying to cool herself. The tiredness and profundity on her face suggests to me that this is how she must look after making love. There is a wisp of hair across her forehead, and her mouth, her elongated mouth, is partially open. Her eyes are looking into the distance, as in a post-coital repose. The sounds conveyed by the arrangement of consonants and vowels in her name, Arancha Sánchez-Vicario, indicate to me what must be the scrumptious dynamic of her lovemaking.

In the same issue is a black and white study of Victoria Cirlot, a professor of Spanish literature. She wants to say that through certain books life can become an ever increasing adventure and a constant search. Well, for me it always has been that way.

Later in the evening, as I walk the promenade with twilight darkening the skies, I notice Jupiter high above the western horizon. This is the planet which shines with a lustre second only to that of Venus, and tonight is almost bright enough to cast a shadow.

Patrick Hewitt was born in Limerick city. He lived in many parts of Ireland before settling in Galway in the mid-1990s. He works as a continuing education facilitator.

Kevin Higgins

Original Bohemian Writes To Ex-Boyfriend About Astronomy

The kitchen's too big and the neighbours are noisier
since the taxi-driver from the Ivory Coast,
I invited back for coffee,
took my Moving Hearts LPs
and vanished into the vast
smoke-free future.

I am a book of complaints
in a town that loves its sushi
and minimalist furniture,
but doesn't do bad news.

This letter is all there is, light
from an extinguished star:
a message reaching you
too late.

Kevin Higgins' first collection of poems, *The Boy With No Face*, was published by Salmon in 2005. Also in 2005, he received a Literature Bursary from the Arts Council and was shortlisted for the Hennessy Award for Poetry. He teaches poetry workshops at Galway Arts Centre and, with his wife Susan Millar DuMars, organises the Over The Edge: Open Reading series in Galway City Library. In February 2006, he did a five-stop reading tour of the US Midwest.

PAUL PERRY

The Lady with the Coronet of Jasmine

I saw her again today.
Graceful in her poverty,
elegant. Her lips a luscious

sanguine escape. A bright
exit. Her tilted head,
diffident, but proud.

She walked past me and I
smelt the fleshly odour
of temptation, heavy

in the air, eager to cling
to me. Her reckless smile
unhinging my composure.

But it cannot be.
It cannot.
It must be that my retirement

from public office is
making me drowsy,
like a summer bee

gorged on honey.
In actuality, it is twenty
years since I have seen her.

A man of my age should
not be given over to fancy,
to frenetic breaths

and tremblings. A man
of my age who at the start
of the century

heard the guns
from Edinburgh Castle
fire announcing

the abdication
of Napoleon and lived
to the end of the century,

I am ripe, and heard
his own voice,
by then a scant baritone

echo of what it once
had been, recorded by
the telephone, should not

indulge in flighty reminiscences.
And yet, memory trawls
my conscious thoughts back

to her, inevitably,
unavoidably, magnetically so.
And should I be so surprised?

A man, that is all I am,
A simple, humble, imperfect man,
a man with a name of more portentousness

than pragmatism. William
Gladstone, a name, a gasp.
I say it to myself and it sounds

from my mouth like the name of a stranger.
I garden. I try to remain calm.
I should make my peace.

But she is there.
In the soil as my fingers dig
for the flowers, she is there

haunting me from the past.
Emily Fenn was to be my saving
grace. An Irish peasant

from the wily shorn land
of Connemara in the West.
Wan refugee from the blighted

island next door. Alone, insomniac
walking the streets and keeping
company with other ladies

of the night time persuasion.
I won't mince my words:
she was a prostitute

And I tried to save her, to rescue
her like so many other girls.
The grimy dirt of night fell around us.

Her voice was soft, plangent
like waves falling onto a shingled beach.
She mistook me for the wrong kind

of gentleman the first time I met her,
entreated me to the squalid
room she shared with her companions.

Her words were timid
and frail like chipped wood.
The misunderstanding over

we talked about her redemption.
I encouraged her to stay
at the House of Mercy on Clewer

and Rose Street in Soho.
But she came back after a week
and said she didn't want to be

locked away like that, that she would
have committed suicide had she stayed.
I calmed her, sat her down. We

entertained long meandering conversations.
I read her Tennyson, which she confessed
to being much impressed by. Indeed

her very shape seemed to waver
in the candle flame and so great
was her sincerity and enthusiasm

in this regard that I actually
gave her my signed copy of *Idylls*
and within a week she had memorised

large sections of the book.
Another day.
It is no good. The calendar is

wearing me away and I can think
of nothing else, but her.
I confess, I went out of duty,

but also out of need.
Light falling on her hands,
elegant and white. My desires grew.

I sought her out. The desire
I felt when I walked the shoddy streets
of London was calamitous.

Desire seethed in I me;
it burned, raged, galloped, slammed,
transported me into all manner

of reverie. Woman. I wanted to enter,
possess, raze and rebuild your
mysterious form. I wanted to enter

your hypnotic realm.
Emily, you represented to me
all the beautiful possibilities

of life and I courted evil
only to overcome it. I went
to her again and again and

because of the hardships she
had endured and the tales of hunger
and desperation she told of her native land,

to say hardship would be an injustice,
it was misery what she described
and all the more for the unpleading manner

she relayed the story of her life,
as if such privation was itself
what God had deemed her and her own

worthy of. Six brothers, three sisters.
Her mother dead. I can hear her voice.
I am happier here, she'd say.

Though, I don't feel like the same person.
I feel like a completely different person.
And eventually I would leave after talking

for so long with the grubby feeling of money
in my hands. My garden does not need
my tending. I sit. Foolishly, I read.

My mind is moidered.
The words on the page are a weak echo
of the other literature I once read.

Books with impure passages,
concealed beneath the veil
of a quite foreign medium,

so I drank the poison, sinfully
because understanding was thus hidden
by a cloud – I have stained my memory

and my soul – which may it please God
to cleanse me, as I have need.
I have read sinfully, although with disgust,

under the pretext of hunting
soberly for what was innocent.
And though today, I read the good book,

Corinthians 10, I am still afflicted
with too many memories.
I read, 'No temptation has seized you

except what is common to man.
And god is faithful; he will not let you
be tempted beyond what you can bear.

But when you are tempted,
he will also provide a way out
so that you can stand up under it'.

But Lord, this is more than I can bear.
Where are you? Answer my prayers.
When I walk those streets again,

admittedly a good deal slower,
I see her. I know it is not her,
but some likeness, some young fresh face

with a halo of jasmine. My mind
is playing tricks. And for a moment
I am happy. I think of the day

she sat for the painting my friend Dyce
composed of her, how he made her
immortal, pure, clean, after

the avaricious attacks of desire
I visited upon her.
She was angelic, fine, the fond
glow from her cheeks forgiving me

and when he asked me to place
the coronet of jasmine
on her, I felt all the humility of a disciple.

The incredulity of Saint Thomas
with his fingers seeking out
the cave of flesh in his chest.

Yes. And yet, I suppose I felt
the guilt of Pontius Pilate.
But what grace the painting lent me.

For in it, she is gazing at me,
the missing subject, the beloved.
And yet, this is the chief burden

of my soul, rending it
to a ragged status. Desire
is gone. Mnemosyne

has chosen her to be my muse.
My wife Catherine is here,
all my loved ones. And yet.

And yet. I remember returning home
time and time again to scourge myself.
The skin on my back blistered and bled

like a hungry map of my misdeeds.
I did not tend to those wounds.
My penance was pain, physical,

self-inflicted, hopeless pain.
Even today I went to find her.
But of course, she was not there.

Only the weak resemblances I am
afraid to converse with.
And if I could find her what would I say?

Our friendship lasted but a year,
before she made her way to America.
Of course, I should have written.

She is surely living a powerful life.
How can I depart this stage
with no fond thought of those around me,

only the desperate recollections
of a short wild passion?
Unkept diaries. And yet,

I think I loved her. What awful
headaches, I've had today.
I go about my chores with the lethargy

of an old man. I sit in the dark
to quell the pain in my head.
And now I have oral hallucinations

to contend with too. My loved
ones turn around me and weep
as if my condition is something

they can do anything about it.
The redemption of these poor creatures
that's what I wanted, now it is my own

salvation that is necessary.
I have set down a black mark
against this day like so many others.

Give me penance O Lord worthy of my sins.
Tomorrow is Sunday.
What kind of atonement can He conjure?

Will he take this emblazoned image
from my mind? As if the woman
with the coronet of jasmine was a curse.

What penance will God find for me?
How will I move from this purgatorial
conflagration? And Lord God, do I deserve to?

Paul Perry was born in Dublin in 1972. He was Writer in Residence for Co. Longford from 2000–2002 and is currently Writer in Residence in the University of Ulster. He won the Hennessy New Irish Writer of the Year Award in 1998 and the Listowel Prize for Poetry in 2002. His first book, *The Drowning of the Saints*, was published in 2003 to critical acclaim; his second, *Wintering*, is published by Dedalus in 2006.

FIONA PLACE

A Journey I Have Taken

When we hear the word journey we usually associate it with a holiday we may have taken or a trip we have been on. I have been on many journeys. I have walked on hot sands, swam in the clear blue ocean, ate pizza in Italy, drank sangria in Spain and rode a donkey up a mountain in Crete.

However, although these journeys were exciting and cultural, those dark feelings always came back. This negative voice telling me 'I'm worthless', the feeling of emptiness and bareness, the looming question in my head saying 'what next?' I have gone from job to job, I have studied and studied some more. I could never settle anywhere in particular. Weekends were daunting because I could not rest. I used to take my daughter everywhere and anywhere in search of some kind of happiness. During the summer I worked in a crèche from Monday to Friday and I worked hard. I played even harder. At night-time my mind would be racing. I could not sleep and when I did my dreams disturbed me. I had Race Week off, and instead of taking it easy, I decided to take my daughter to Tramore for a few days. However I was not well and those days were a disaster for me. I could not return to work – they were letting me go at the end of August anyway. I used the rest of the summer to spend time with my daughter and sending CV after CV to companies.

I was tired, I had no appetite. I was feeling worthless and I lost interest in everything. The more rejections I got the more I sunk further into the ground. Nevertheless, I was not rooted, I was scattered. I had no focus but I did not want to think and assess myself. I kept going and kept moving until finally, when my daughter returned to school I crashed. There was pressure in my head, I wanted to kill myself, but would not do that to my daughter. Alcohol was making me more depressed. I knew there was something wrong.

That's when my journey began. When I crashed I finally opened my eyes. I looked deep into my soul and realized I did not know who I was. My whole life had been a façade. This journey has not been easy. The road is treacherous. There are ups and there are downs, sometimes I see things clearly and sometimes I can't see at all. It can be very hard looking deep inside yourself. In order to make a change, habits of a lifetime have to be broken. The day-to-day routine suddenly has to be assessed and questions need to be asked. Sometimes I think that it would be easier to go back to my old ways, pretending things are ok, work in jobs that are below my capabilities and go back to relationships that are not good for my being. However, I will not do that. I will travel this treacherous road and when I finally reach my destination I will know that this journey was worth taking.

Some people might say I had a breakdown, I prefer to call it a breakthrough ...

Fiona Place took part in a creative writing workshop with Máire Holmes in Galway Arts Centre. She lives in Galway.

Maram al-Massri

Every night the birds sleep in their solitude

Translated from the French
by Charlotte Mandell

Every night the birds sleep in their solitude
They look at their bodies as if they were a woman's body,
Frail, but with it they fight the wind and the water

Every night
The birds and the bears dream of hands stroking them

Cats stretch out to lick their fur never
Worrying about the god's eyes scattered all over the ceiling and walls
Never worrying about gossip
Or the judges or the prisons of love
Or the mandibles of moths devouring the garments of desire

They're happy being themselves
In the quiet of their body
Full of joy they breathe in
the morning

Maram al-Massri was born in Latakia, Syria and has lived in France since 1982. She has published three collections in Arabic, and her poems have been translated into many languages. Her bilingual English-Arabic edition, *A Red Cherry on a White-tiled Floor: Selected Poems*, translated by Khaled Mattawa, was published by Bloodaxe in 2004.

Abdelwahab Meddeb

Wandering

Translated from the French
by Charlotte Mandell

To leave with nothing except maybe under your arm
the Book what's the use if its words lodge at the bottom
of the heart unless you repair the holes
of memory opening up sewn bound notebooks
you will not burden yourself with the weight of statues
even if they're made of a marble whose shadow meets
the gold of icons stretching beyond the angle that wounds
you will reproduce your columns at every stop
by cloistering the open space that welcomes you with stones
you will gather on your way among the pebbles
of the shore or when you dig into the desert mesas
will you know how to invent the image that will give
the thuja argan that shape of a cherry tree whose flowers
catch on your eyelashes before they fly above
people's heads to join the clouds mirage
the instant the flakes from one climate to the other
cross the front of the island that the fog from the east
brings on the waves come from the horizon that
the night slips on to go hem the foam
where the thornbushes wash themselves before
unfurling army of hairy dwarfs brandishing spears
whose tips riddle the skin with black spots
web of a sieve that a quiet sun burns

without any fuss the salty weathered body is given
over to the power of Eros who provokes the cry
mingling with the voice of the noonday call
song coming from a village you can't see
that skims the music of the bells on the necks
of the goats the patriarch herds his sleepy eyes
are mirrored in the folds of his tunic eyes
veiled by the rivalry of the skies the shepherd
lets his arms swing slung over the staff
borne on the nape of the neck the ridge of his shoulders
gesture that carries back to ancient times
traces of a language whose sounds I would
have to taste if I wanted to sew up the gash
where the garden of nakedness was left forever

Abdelwahab Meddeb was born in Tunis in 1946 and has lived in Paris since 1968. He is a poet, novelist, translator and essayist and is the editor of the journal *Dédale*. He was the currator of the 2005 exhibition 'west by east' for the Centre of Contemporary Culture in Barcelona which brought together ancient and contemporary artworks relating to Western society from the Arab world. He is the author of twenty books and is Professor of Comparative Literature at the University of Paris X-Nanterre.

EOIN COLFER

A Fowl Tale

In medieval Europe, travellers were always welcome to a bowl of stew on one condition-they were required to spin an interesting tale. On this occasion an unusual traveller joins the queue of Erik the Boy King.

Finally, it was my turn to speak. And a good thing too because I was famished. I'll just spin them my yarn, I thought. Whatever it takes to get a bowl of stew, and maybe a good deal more.

'You there', said the boy king, pointing the sword at the knight below me. 'Tell us a tale'.

'Just a minute', I protested swooping down to the table. 'I believe *I* am next'.

The assembly *was* surprised to hear a bird speak, but I didn't get the big reaction I usually get. Generally there are cries of *aaarrgh*! *Witchcraft!* And *boil the demon chicken*. But this time, just a few raised eyebrows. I suppose after the stories already told this day, the assembly has become accustomed to the fantastic.

I fluffed my feathers. 'Well? Do I get my rightful turn? Will you deny a bird his feed?'

The boy king smiled. 'Proceed, Master Chicken'.

'I am not a chicken', I said, feeling slightly miffed. 'I am a dove. It's a completely different thing. Pigeons are dirty creatures who chatter incessantly and deposit their droppings on whatever patch of ground they happen to be inhabiting. We doves are far more discreet'.

'Accept my humble apologies and pray proceed, Master Dove'.

I bowed in thanks. Now for my story. Not mine, of course. There must be one

I could drag up from childhood memories. I would make them drag mine from me.

'Ahem, yes. My story. Once there was a noble knight who searched far and wide for the holy grail'.

A noble knight behind me in the queue raised a chain-mailed finger.

'That would be me, and that would be my story'.

I changed tack hurriedly. 'On a fine Summer's day three little pigs decided to move out of their mother's house …'

'Heard it', said the boy king.

I tried again. 'One morning, a lonely orphan received his invitation to attend wizard school …'

The boy's sword quivered a hair's breadth from my beak. 'The line is long, bird. Tell your tale or forfeit your meal'.

I tried to make light of the situation. 'There are only seven real stories anyway. What matter the tale, as long as it is well told?'

'There is only one story here and now, Master Dove', said the boy king, frowning. 'And that is yours. Are you willing to share it?'

I snapped at an impertinent flea between my feathers. 'The whole affair is a tad embarrassing. Not something one likes to talk about in polite society'.

The knight chortled. 'One talks about? Polite society? You're very well spoken, for a chicken'.

'Dove!' I snapped. 'And yes, polite society. I am after all royalty. Or I was, until I was transformed.

The knight elbowed a hermit beside him. 'Don't tell me, you're the missing Prince Husnivarr'.

I didn't answer, just clicked my beak modestly.

The knight drummed his fingers on an armoured forearm. 'So, you're saying, little chicken, that you *are* Prince Husnivarr? Heir to the Mont Varr kingdom, not to mention the mountain of gold. But every one knows that the Husnivarr brat was transformed into a pig'.

'That is so untrue', I chirped. 'Well, perhaps I was something of a brat, but I was *never* a pig. Never. There was a pig in the vicinity when my transformation took place, and it caused some confusion, that's all'.

'Whatever you say, porky', said the knight, winking at the assembly. I was really beginning to dislike that man.

'Speak, Prince', said the boy king, interrupting the general laughter. 'Your own story this time'.

It was time for my story. It was that or hunger.

'It *is* true', I began sadly. 'I am Prince Husnivarr, or rather I was. This poor battered bird you see before you was once the heir to the richest kingdom on earth. I lived a priviliged life in court. My duties were light and my comforts were many. I grew spoilt and petulant. My father, a noble king, decided that a good old fashioned task would strengthen my character. One day he called me into his throne room and sat me by his side.

'One day the big chair will be yours, Husni', he said. 'And I don't think that you have the bottom to fill it. I've been watching lately, and you have no respect for your fellow man or beast. You need to learn that respect before you can be king'.

There was a golden tray on his knee and on the tray rested a common grey rock. It was about the size of a rabbit's head and streaked with white.

'This is the Karma Stone', my father explained. 'My magicians brought it back from Persia. We had to dig a large chunk from the mountain of gold to pay for it'.

'Very, eh, pretty', I said, reaching to stroke the stone.

'Not so eager, Husnivarr', said the king, grasping my wrist. 'The Karma Stone moves anyone who touches it through their circle of life. It accelerates their incarnations. Watch'.

My father placed his hand on the stone and immediately transformed. He became a stoat, then a wolf, a tall shaggy beast that I could not identify and then, once more, himself. Finally, he removed his hand.

'You get what you deserve, you see. It only took me three incarnations to become a man. Strength of character, you see. And when I die, I will become a stoat once more. You, Husni, I suspect it will take you a thousand years to become human again. Would you like to know how many stages there will be for you?'

'No', I replied.

'I insist', said my father, placing my hand on the Karma Stone.

My transformation was immediate. The world grew huge as I grew small, and only my human thought process kept me from flying away. I was a mosquito.

'Aah', said my gigantic father mournfully. 'It is worse than I thought. You will begin your next cycle as a mosquito. Very low on the reincarnation scale'.

The urge to suck his blood quickly faded, as I transformed into a dung beetle.

'Still an insect', noted the king. 'I hope you become a mammal soon, for your mother's sake'.

My shell popped and disappeared, fur sprouted along my back and I became a rat. I could clearly see my own nose and the whiskers quivering like tiny foils at its tip.

'A mammal', admitted my father. 'But not a very noble one'.

Then disaster struck. A crazed pig, escaped from the kitchen, burst into the chamber, pursued by a trio of cleaver wielding butchers. Pandemonium was immediate. I was in the throes of becoming a dove, and could barely follow the sequence of events.

The pig charged my father's chair, knocking him over backwards to the floor. His head cracked against the stone flags, knocking the life from his body. My contact with the Karma Stone was roughly broken before my human senses had asserted themselves. I had become a dove, with a dove's brain and vocabulary. The pig lunged, the butchers swiped their cleavers and I flew. Oink, roar and coo!

I followed my dove's instincts and found an open window. In minutes I was miles away, riding the tails of a westbound wind. For two years I roamed the skies as a simple dove, with no inkling of what had befallen me. Until one Summer, I made my home in the eaves of a cottage and heard human voices once more. These voices stirred something within me, waking memories and senses.

I realised that I must return immediately to my grieving family, and assure them that their son and heir is alive and well, if a little indisposed. Once they hear what my late father did to me, I feel sure that I will be welcomed with open wings, eh, arms. So that is my quest, and I have only stopped here for a much needed meal'.

I finished my tale, dipping my beak in a convenient water jug. My story had been a success. Already the waiter was filling a bowl of stew.

The knight removed his helmet. 'A fascinating story, chicken. Prince Husnivarr you say?'

'Alas, yes', I said. Sad yet noble.

'Amazing. The Karma Stone, you say?'

I snapped my beak. 'Yes, yes. That's what happened'.

The knight removed one gauntlet. 'And tell me, chicken … I mean, Prince, about your famous family birthmark'.

Birthmark? I had a famous birthmark?

'Ah, yes. Of course. The heirs to the mountain of gold, always have a birthmark, in the shape of a … birthmark. The exact details escape me at the moment. Not all my memories have returned'.

The knight peeled off his breastplate. 'Let me refresh your memory. The birthmark is in the shape of a peacock's fan. Rather like this one'.

There was a birthmark on the knight's side, in the shape of a peacock's fan.

I flapped my wings nervously. 'So, that would mean, that you would be …'

'Prince Husnivarr', completed the knight. 'I've been away on a campaign. Not a pig or chicken in sight'.

'This is ridiculous', I blustered. 'I am Husnivarr, rightful heir to the …'

'Mountain of gold', completed the knight. 'More of a molehill I'm afraid. Oh, it was a mountain once, but that was before empire tax and a few decades of war. I'd be surprised if there's a single sovereign left in the treasury now'.

I felt like fainting. 'No gold?'

'Not a penny'.

'There's still the castle', I said, grasping at straws.

'There is that', agreed the knight. 'A fine castle with portraits of me in every hall'.

'Ah …' I could feel all eyes on me now. 'Perhaps I exaggerated my story slightly'.

The boy king drew his sword again. 'So, you're not a magical dove'.

'No. A parrot actually. An albino parrot'.

'And how did you learn to talk'.

'I always knew how to talk. But I learned to understand in a magician's laboratory. Some chap called Marvin, I think'.

'Merlin?' said the boy.

'That's the one. I think breathing in the gas from his potions boosted my parrot brain somewhat'.

The knight broke the tension. He laughed until his armour rattled and salty tears gathered in his beard.

'By God, a conniving parrot. I've heard it all now. I want to thank you, little chicken. I haven't laughed this much in a decade. Not since I was turned into a pig'.

They were all laughing now, and I sensed that a meal might still be on offer. I waved a wing towards the steaming pot.

'I've told you a story, do I get a bowl? Just a small one. I eat like a bird'.

The knight snatched a bowl from a passing steward. 'Of course, young prince. Your lies are worth at least a few chunks of boiled meat'.

I peered into the bowl. The soup was grey and unappealing.

'And what meat would that be?' I asked.

Prince Husnivarr winked maliciously.

'Chicken', he replied.

Eoin Colfer was a primary school teacher in Wexford when he cast a spell on the publishing and film industries with his fantastically original novel, *Artemis Fowl*. His first novel, *Benny and Omar* was an instant success in Ireland, even knocking Harry Potter off the number one spot for best-selling children's books. Like *Artemis Fowl* it was written after a day's teaching and after his son's bedtime. Total sales of Eoin's *Artemis Fowl* titles now exceed 1.6 million copies in the UK and Ireland, and over 6 million worldwide.

Tanya Farrelly

Whiteout

Lucille left one cold night in December. Her departure was not planned. It was something done in haste, as many things in Lucille's life were. That night, she had gone to the theatre. She had asked Eugene to accompany her. He was too busy, he said. She did not mind. She was accustomed to Eugene's refusal, particularly of late, when it seemed impossible to persuade him out of doors. Besides she liked to go out alone. It gave her an air of mystery.

It was late when she got home. He had left the light on downstairs for her. It shone through the hall window, illuminated the concrete figures in the neighbour's garden, lending them a somewhat eerie appearance, like apparitions, white and still. Lucille pulled into the garage. She switched the engine off, and rummaged in her bag for the key. She opened the door and stepped into the hall. She plucked at the fingers of her leather gloves, and unwound the scarf from around her neck. She hung her red coat on the end of the bannister, sat on the stairs, and pulled her boots off.

She wondered whether Eugene had gone to bed. She felt a thrill at the prospect. She would creep upstairs, slip beneath the covers, and wake him to make love. It was a game they often played. In the dark she could be anyone. Her lips travelling down his body could be that of a stranger. She thought of him, stirring in half-sleep, his body responding to her touch. The thought that it might not be her partner in bed, but that it might be a complete stranger was an erotic if slim possibility. Lucille had a taste for the dramatic.

She laid her keys and bag on the living room table, where an open bottle of red wine stood, uncorked. Beside it, a glass that was not quite empty. Lucille raised the glass and drained it. Her lipstick stained the rim red. She poured herself another, lingered in the living room. She sat on the sofa, and put her feet up on the wooden table. It was a good show. She was sorry that Eugene had not gone with her. He liked that type of thing. Lately, all he ever seemed to do was work. Still, once the book was finished, she supposed, everything could get back to normal.

Lucille finished her wine. She left her glass on the table, and turned the light out. Slowly she climbed the stairs. The bedroom door was closed. She eased it open and stepped inside. Eugene's shaving lotion spiked the air. She guessed that he was not long gone to bed. In the dark she undressed, hung her clothes over the arm of the bedroom chair.

'How was the show?'

She was surprised when he spoke. She figured that he would be asleep, or pretending to be asleep.

'It was good, very good. You'd have liked it', she said.

Lucille stood on one foot, then the other, as she peeled off her tights, and flung them on the chair. She slipped beneath the covers. Eugene's body was warm. His hair was damp from the shower. She waited for him to turn toward her. When he didn't, she wondered whether he had fallen asleep. She began to feel slightly annoyed. Not only had her fantasy been dashed, he made no attempt to touch her. She lay on her back. There was a gap between their bodies, which she refused to close. Eugene had pulled the pillows down at the angle, and was curled away toward the wall. Cold crept beneath the covers. She sighed. She was tired, and irritable.

'I was talking to Amy'.

Eugene's voice rang out in the silence. He was not asleep after all.

'Oh. How is she?'

'She's fine'. He paused. 'I told her to come over at the weekend'.

'What's she coming over here for?' she said.

The words came out before she could stop them. She hated this, hated the way that she sounded, even though she knew that she had good reason. She always ended up sounding unreasonable, irrational even. And she hated that.

'Are you in a mood?'

He hadn't moved. His words were muffled beneath the blankets.

'No. I'm just asking what she's coming over here for, that's all'.

'Why wouldn't she?' he asked.

She lay on her back, her eyes adjusted now to the darkness.

'Well, you needn't expect me to entertain her', she said.

'Nobody's expecting you to do anything'.

And that was that. Lucille waited, thinking that maybe he still might turn toward her. She wouldn't touch him, not now. She would not make the first move. She lay on her back, and waited. He said nothing more. In the silence her irritation grew. It was fuelled by the fact that he did nothing to pacify her, nothing to comfort her. She thought that the move to Edmonton might have changed things. That the distance might have proved too great for their friendship to endure.

She lay there and wondered what to do. She couldn't sleep. Her mind was too active. She wished that he would say something. Anything. That way they could have it out, and be done with it. Eugene said nothing. Lucille turned over, widening the void. She could sleep downstairs, she supposed, on the sofa. That would make a statement. Or she could leave. The thought occurred to her suddenly. She didn't know why. But now that it had occurred she couldn't rest easy. She felt that she had no choice. That is why she would do it - she would leave. It wouldn't get that far anyway. Eugene would ask her what she was doing as soon as he heard her stumbling around in the dark. He would tell her not to be foolish, to come back to bed. Eugene was practical like that.

Lucille slipped from beneath the covers. She sat on the edge of the bed. She was tired. Too tired for such foolishness. She stood up. She tripped on his boots in the dark, and cursed softly. That would wake him, if he were not still awake. She took her clothes from the bedroom chair. She dressed, and fumbled on the floor for her shoes. She sat on the edge of the bed. Still, he said nothing. Lucille hesitated. Was he asleep after all? Time was running out. Maybe she should get undressed, slip into bed, and say nothing, but she had come this far.

She stood up; noisily she opened the bedroom door. The figure beneath the clothes did not stir. She closed the door behind her, and crept down the stairs. She stopped in the hall, sat down on the bottom step of the stairs, and waited. The only sound was the ticking of the clock. God, she was tired. Her eyes burned when she closed them. Perhaps she would go for a walk as far as the garden gate. She dare not go any further, not with the forecast.

She took her keys from the table, and opened the front door. Moonlight filled the hallway. Lucille stepped outside, and pulled the door behind her. It was cold. Damn cold. Frost shimmered dangerously on the pavement. The snow had not yet come. She moved her feet, rubbed her arms. She watched the front door. It remained maddeningly closed. Then she had an idea.

She opened the garage door, unlocked the car, and sat into the driver's seat. She put the key in the ignition. What if he looked out, and the car was gone? He would be frantic. He would come after her surely? What man wouldn't? And so Lucille had her plan. She would drive to the end of the road and stop there. She would wait a few minutes. That was all it would take for him to arrive.

She started the engine. She turned the heater on and gripped the wheel. She reversed out of the drive and put the car into gear. Slowly she pulled away from the house. She glanced in the rear view mirror. Nothing stirred. She rounded the bend, continued on a couple of blocks, then pulled in. She turned the lights off, but left the engine running. There was nobody around. Houses were in darkness, their inhabitants fast asleep in bed. Lucille looked at the sky. A full moon illuminated the night. A cat streaked across the road and disappeared into somebody's garden. Suddenly she felt alone. She locked the car doors and sat back in her seat. Every so often she glanced up the road.

Lucille switched the radio on. She drummed her fingers on the steering wheel. She was beginning to feel foolish. What must he think, after all? She wondered about Amy. Had she phoned? Had he phoned her? What difference did it make? She had taken a dislike to the woman. It wasn't the fact that they were close, though that did have something to do with it. She couldn't stand her whining voice. The way she pawed him when she spoke. He, of course, never noticed. Or he pretended not to. They had been friends for years, he and Amy. She was the first girl he had slept with. A brief adolescent fling — it was something that Amy liked to joke about in an all too innocent way. It made Lucille smoulder.

She looked at the dashboard. The needle on the fuel gauge hovered just above empty. The yellow warning light was on. Her eyes were heavy with sleep. She flicked through the radio channels, looked for something that might keep her awake until he came. 'Minus thirty-eight degrees tonight in Edmonton, and falling', she was in time to hear the announcer say. She turned the heat up. In the mirror she saw a car approaching. The lights vanished at the bend, then reappeared. Her heart quickened. The car approached slowly. She waited for the driver to indicate and pull in. Instead they drove on. Lucille slumped forward in her seat, gripped the steering wheel and laid her head against her hands. The engine spluttered, then died. She tried to start it. It moaned. The yellow light blinked at her.

Cold crept into the car and she tightened her scarf beneath her collar. Her fingers were numb in the leather gloves. She wriggled them, rubbed her hands together in an attempt to circulate the blood. She thought of Eugene, his body warm against hers, as they lay parallel between the sheets. She shivered and drew her coat closer round her. There was not a sound. Not a sign of life. Lucille watched the road. A flake drifted and stuck to the windscreen. It was followed by another. Soon it began to come down heavy. Snowflakes whirled and stuck to the glass. She turned the wipers on. She couldn't see a damn thing. She could not feel her feet now. Her cuffs were pulled over her hands. Every so often she thought she heard a car and glanced eagerly toward the bend. Lights appeared in the distance and vanished. Lucille's eyes closed. It became more of an effort to open them each time. Her lids were heavy. Her head drifted sideways, rested against the window. She was vaguely aware of the cold glass against her skin, like metal. Lucille waited. Her eyes closed. This time she did not bother to open them. She was tired. Too tired for such foolishness. Lucille slept. Eugene dreamed. The forecaster's voice crackled over the airwaves. Whiteout.

Tanya Farrelly was born in Dublin in 1977. She is currently studying for a BA Honours Degree in Literature at Dublin Business School. Credits to date include shortlisted for the Hennessy Awards, and RTE's Francis MacManus Awards. Her work has also been published in *Whispers and Shouts* literary journal, and has been broadcast on RTE's Sunday Miscellany. Recently she won second prize in the Edgeworthstown short story competition.

TERESA DAVEY

The Hand of God

David knew he was not alone when the pigeon landed stunned at his feet. Startled he looked up into the sky and recognised the dark shape of a peregrine falcon circling high above. Only last week he'd heard it said by some geek on Radio 4 that if a penny dropped from the Eiffel Tower it would slice into the ground. The image of such a happening kept popping into his head over the following days and he shivered with the realisation that a more offbeat experiment had almost taken place.

The day had been hot, too hot to have toiled to the top of a mountain unless you were a man with a mission. His friends had told him it was a day for the beach, or sitting in the garden of a pub, chilling out. But he was looking for enlightenment and doubted it would present itself in such places. The bible was to blame. The story of the devil offering Christ dominion of the whole world from a mountain top had made such places special in the minds of men. Yet today, like many another, when he looked down from the summit all he'd seen was a beautiful landscape.

Now, on the lower slopes of the mountain, sitting beside a lough where he had stopped to cool off with a swim, contact had finally been made. Naked, wet and a little burned from his long day in the open air, he told himself the peregrine falcon was a messenger from a higher power. In all that large expanse of wilderness he had at last been acknowledged and like Saul on the road to Damascus, it had come when he'd least expected it.

When the stunned pigeon stumbled to its feet at the waters edge his eyes searched it for sign of injury. No blood oozed from its mouth, no wing lurched haphazardly at an odd angle and it managed to perch shakily on two undamaged feet. He decided he should take the pigeon to a fancier who could look after it but when he tried to catch the bird, it had recovered enough to scuttle this way and that just out of reach. One last rescue attempt caused it to fly off close to the ground and take cover in the heather and scrub that grew all over the surrounding hillside.

As he drove home his mind went over the event in greater detail, he imagined a different scenario and smiled. His body found, a pigeon dead beside it. Surely if he was dead the pigeon would be dead. His skull was after all somewhat harder than the weedy water that had cushioned the pigeon's fall. He visualised newspaper headlines 'Death falls from the sky', 'Mystery by the Lonely Lough', 'Bird kills man'. He looked forward to telling his mates over a pint, of his weird near death experience.

That evening his sister gave him an aspirin for his aching head and sent him to bed. As he tried to focus on the familiar walls of his room, a hand, the texture of cloud, came through the window and hovered over his resting body. He heard the Geordie tones of Big Brother saying 'Would David Brown please come to the diary room'. The hand transported him gently to that famous chair. Looking around the enclosed space his eyes focused upon a lectern positioned a little to the left of him on which sat a large bible.

David cleared his throat in order to speak clearly. 'Hello Big Brother'.

'How are you David?'

'Confused, Big Brother'.

There was a short silence before the Geordie tones continued. 'David, my son, you are the chosen one. Will you do as I ask?'

As the pronouncement uncurled itself inside his head, David felt himself glow with pleasure. Unable to speak, he swallowed hard and inclined his head.

'You must follow the road until you see a tree laden with red blossom. In a ditch nearby you will find a saw. Cut the tree down. Cut the branches into logs and use them to warm my needy sheep, those who lay hungry and cold in a dilapidated house, close to flowing water.

Without any awareness of getting there, or the measurement of passing time, David stood beside the tree. Ankle deep in fallen blossom and disorientated from its heady scent he set about his task. He sweated over his labour for several days and slept beside the growing pile of logs. He pushed from his head the knowledge that wood needed to season before it would burn well. If Big Brother wanted it to burn then it would. When he finished his task he packed a haversack that sat nearby with logs and set off to find the needy sheep.

Soon, he was surprised to find himself approaching the village where he'd grown up. Although his watch told him it was midday the streets were empty.

He stopped at the bakery on the main street, where as a young boy he'd been sent by his mother to buy pastries for unexpected visitors. He hadn't been told to feed the sheep but wondered whether he should use his initiative.

'Do you know of a dilapidated house full of cold and hungry sheep?' he asked Mary the buxom cake shop owner, a woman who normally had a cheery 'how are you dear' for everyone.

Mary did not answer but instead cut a large slice of black forest gateau and stuffed it into her mouth. Before he could ask if she had anything past its sell by date, daggers of flame shot out of her eyes, horns pushed up through her hair and levitating from behind the counter, she pointed the long chocolate covered knife at him before her body began to spin. With an icy shiver running up and down his spine David backed out of the shop.

Further down the road, standing outside another shop, he watched as old Mr. Savage the butcher swallowed handfuls of chopped liver, the blood oozing down his chin. The carcass of a dead cow was hanging from the ceiling behind him. Shuddering, David turned away and walked quickly down the road.

At the fishmongers, Delia Moon, the daughter of the owner, a girl he had once dated for several months, leered at him. Wearing a necklace of gaping fish heads, she was cutting the tentacles from a giant octopus. Seeing David looking at her she smiled and wriggled provocatively. The fish heads winked at him evilly as the octopus slipped from her hand. Terrified, he rushed off down the road, leaving his initiative behind.

With the town out of view, David found himself in the garden of a wreck of a house. A wide river flowed nearby. Pushing open the rotted door, a large number of scrawny sheep stared at him from where they lay shivering on the dirty floor. Turning his back on them he opened his backpack and filled the fireplace with logs. Finding matches in his hand he struck one, immediately a fire burned and the room was warm. Hearing a commotion he turned around to find the sheep had been transformed. Standing upright, their shoulders now muscled like those of strong weightlifting men they were jostling each other for a prime fireside position. Scared of being trampled, David slipped outside and walked down to the river. Climbing inside a rowing boat that rocked gently in shallow water, he lay down. As the boat moved into the centre of the river, David drifted into sleep.

When he woke everything was clean and bright and in the distance figures shimmered as they went about their business. A shape emerged from the dazzle and came towards him. It crossed his mind that he'd been transported to heaven as a reward for succeeding in his task and that he was about to be welcomed by an angel. The being took his hand and held his wrist.

'How's the head this morning, mountain man?'

The gravelly voice and sarcasm didn't fit with his idea of an angel. Agitated, he tried to pull his hand away.

'Where's Big Brother? I want to see Big Brother? Where is he?'

'I don't know about Big Brother love. You're in hospital. Your sister brought you in with a bad case of sunstroke, said you were raving about being the chosen one and birds falling from the sky. We had to sedate you'.

David screwed his eyelids together and tried to extricate a straightforward thought from the jumble that were stuck together inside his head. Feeling as though he was about to vomit he opened his eyes to look for a bowl. Davina McCall was standing over him a peregrine falcon on her wrist. As the falcon's long sharp beak punctured the skin of his arm he heard her say.

'Don't worry love, this will make you sleep'.

Teresa Davey has lived in Newcastle, Co. Down for the past twelve years. A member of the Queen's University Belfast Writers' Group, she has had poetry and short stories published in various publications. Most recently two of her stories appear in *The Barefoot Nuns of Barcelona*, an anthology of the winning and shortlisted stories in the Orange Northern Woman short story competition. She has written two novels and is looking for an agent.

Mary O'Donoghue

Fowlers

They traipse into the back yard with their brand-new green wellingtons folded down from the top. They wear tweed caps pulled low on their foreheads. Sean Connery in *The Untouchables.* Their colours are green and brown. Tweedy clothes, town-trying-to-be-country. Holiday-clean, and touristy, they look; nobody round here would be caught dead in a tweed jacket with leather elbow patches. I imagine that they smell of Lifebuoy soap and tobacco.

They cross our farm and go through the wood during four weekends in September and October. The wood has a floor of mossy stones that nuzzle my sandaled feet when I walk there in search of safe-to-eat mushrooms. Green fur that makes me want to lay down and sleep on it. It's the best thing about the land we own, though Finbar is every year talking about 'bulldozing that fucker's fuck of a witch's wood up above the top field'. I tell him that it would bring bad luck to do that. 'It's a fairy wood'. He looks at me like I've spoken in a foreign language. It's the same way he looks at me when I say something romantic. 'My big strong Finbar. You look like Pierce Brosnan in that suit'. I might as well be speaking in tongues, as far as he's concerned. But you have to make an effort to romance your husband. Flatter him every so often, in the hope that he'll give you what you want.

This is the third year of fowlers with guns folded like dancers' skinny legs over their arms. Finbar lets them come in and shoot on our land, for what he calls 'a goodly sum'. This year, I've decided to make a bit of lunch for them. Finbar's after raising the price, and the fowlers can't say a thing about it, because they aren't supposed to be there. 'And there're frig all places they can go looking for the amount of birdies they want, so they'll pay up'. I want to show them that we're decent people, in spite of Finbar's greed for their wad of money. I buy the ingredients for soup, which I've never made in my life, and three types of cheese, and rosemary ham. I follow recipes clipped from magazines. The recipes tell you the calorie count and all that rubbish, but all I want to do is to make something that'll have the men breathing satisfaction round the kitchen, apologizing after their burps, asking for more. Looking at me like they'd swap their own women in a second.

I decide to change my clothes while the soup is thickening, and come back downstairs in black jeans and the sleeveless silvery blouse that tightens and chafes against my shoulders. It feels like tinsel on my skin, and it reminds me to walk tall. A line from a poem comes into my head: something-something-something, 'and she walked the walk of a queen'. I let an invisible string draw me up to my full height, like the wedding etiquette book advised.

I tell Finbar's sister that he's 'taking his sweet time to give me children'. This, as we sit at a table at his youngest brother's wedding. In front of us, rinds of ham and cigarettes crushed out on potato skins. Eimear tells me that the bride is, 'you know…', and she moves her hands over her stomach, making a hemisphere, 'but, sure, not so's you notice, and who's counting these days, anyhow?' She calls out to her own two, twin boy and girl, kneeling over another seven-year-old cousin, pouring Fanta orange into his mouth as he lies on the carpet like a little corpse decked out in a pressed trousers and waistcoat. Even the bottoms of his shoes are pristine, their skin-coloured soles with the maker's name embossed so clearly I could read it. *Dubarry.*

'Brian! Elva! Get UP from that, and leave that poor child alone, or do I have to come over there? DO I?' Eimear glares them into getting up and pulling their cousin up from the floor. Orange dribbles from the corner of his mouth, and he looks pleased with himself for surviving the ordeal, and drinking a shitload of Fanta into the bargain. All the kids at the wedding glug back pint glasses of Coke and red lemonade. They ram their hands into crisp packets and split them open to get the last few crumbs. They're delirious with the amount of stuff they trick adults into buying for them. Kids are great like that. Pure opportunists.

As I watch them in little gangs round the dance-floor, the feeling of fists starts up inside my chest. My eyes blur. It's happening more and more often. Lately, buggies in town bring it on. Those huge buggies that make babies look like they're tucked inside a space-craft. 'The Massey Ferguson tractor', as my sister Dot's husband calls theirs, steering it into our kitchen, searching for a space to park it. Dot tells us about the mothers in New York who have three-wheeled buggies, for pushing while they're jogging.

'All the gear, mind you. Runners and headbands and their ponytails swinging behind them. And the baby out in front, bombing it at fifty miles an hour. That's why they're not called 'strollers' any more. Jesus Christ; d'you think I went out jogging after I had this one? Did I, frig!'

She leans down, eye-level with small Evan. I have to get up from the table, for fear of making a show of myself.

After that, I can't stop thinking about being out the country roads, running with a baby in a buggy like that. Pounding the road past the bog, loving the baby's head peeping from a hood out in front of me. But, of course, you can't do that around here. You'd either get mown down by some young lunatic in a tractor, or you'd be told by your husband that it wasn't 'the done thing', as Finbar once said to me. About lying at the lake with my bikini straps untied to get a better tan on my back. I was there by myself, reading a book about women in the French Resistance. Must've been someone passing who saw me, and likely dropped it on Finbar on a night at the pub. 'You might want to warn that wife-een of yours …'

I take my glass and chuck the Bailey's back my throat, then I tell Eimear about Finbar and children. She doesn't know where to look or what to say. I want to tell her that I love Finbar as I'm sure she and her other two sisters did when they were small girls. Older, bigger, clumsier, lovable in his complete pig-ignorance to the smell of farm rolling off him, the iodine-and-milk smell of the parlour. Lovable in that he had to be looked after; in how easy it is to please him with a ham sandwich made with thick batch bread.

I stand up and turn for the Ladies'. I use the red flowers patterning the carpet to make sure I walk a straight line; I know Eimear is watching my back. And I know she won't say a thing more about what I've told her. She'll blame it on the drink, and never think about it again.

True to form. The cut of Finbar.

Whatever you say, say nothing.

Aren't we better off not talking ourselves to death about it.

We'll take it handy and see what happens.

What happens is that I dab Chanel behind my ears and hope that the smell of the soup won't cover it up. I've followed a recipe for seafood bisque; it's a lovely pink porridge of a soup.

What happens is that I ladle it into the bowl of the green-eyed man from Wicklow town, the one who came last year, and made a thing of chatting to me while Finbar inspected the cheque the other man gave him, and into the bowl of his shooting partner.

'Yes', I told him last year, in a hurtle of words, 'I do have a little part-time job. At a school. I supervise study from four until six'.

The man from Wicklow town eats the soup carefully, and doesn't rattle the spoon against his teeth like Finbar does. You can make a fool of yourself by wearing a sleeveless silver blouse, by keeping your arms close to your sides, soldier-stiff, so the men in your kitchen can't see the sweat tarnishing the silver under your arms. *A horse sweats; a man perspires; a woman merely glows.* Bullshit to that, you think.

You can make a fool of yourself by spending two hours picking out the fish for pulverizing into bisque, by putting on a posh voice when you ask for 'mossels', and the fishmonger up to his wrists in green fish-heads gives you a look that says, *what's this guff talk ? Don't I know you, in here every second Friday for mackerel ?* The dirtiest fish in the sea.

Spritzing yourself with perfume that belongs to a wedding or a night out at a restaurant, and not in a kitchen with soup in the air and men that smell like wet leaves and axle grease.

And you can make a right fool of yourself – what your brother might call 'a right tit of yarself' – by waiting for one of these men, these men with their guns ready to bring down birds from the sky, waiting for one of them to look at you the way that reminds you that you still have soft white hands, in spite of the farm, and hair that holds onto the smell of apple shampoo. And a stomach that's stayed as flat as it was when you were a teenager.

The man from Wicklow collects the last of the bisque on his spoon and raises it to me like he's making a toast. 'This is grand soup. Like something you'd get in a restaurant isn't it, Padraig?' Padraig is already out of his chair, picking up his gun. 'Oh, it is. Great grub altogether, ma'am. We'll have to come back'.

Bellies full, they swing out into the yard. Through the window, I hear them snap their guns together. It's a satisfying sound, quick and business-like. Through the red gate they go, up the field, aiming for the wood. I think of the moss being crushed under their wellingtons, birds routed from the undergrowth at the sound of their steps. There's something stunning about the sight of a shoot. The arc of the bird's path; the sudden halt like it's crashed into a window in the sky. The way it falls like a neat little bundle. Because suddenly it has weight, and the ground is hauling it down. Plucked pheasants remind me of the rough skin under Finbar's chin. The smell of plucking is old Christmases, and home, and my mother tugging feathers from a goose. The sound of the thick pink skin reluctantly giving up those feathers was always louder than I expected. It was the same sound as when I pinched balloons, daring them not to burst.

And on the far side of the farm, Finbar, mending walls. Wearing those huge cloth gloves that make his hands look like a clown's hands. He has no real bad in him; I know that. And I should be glad of it. I feel sorry at the thought of him coming back to the kitchen. Getting the smell of strange soup, wondering why there's none left for him.

Mary O'Donoghue grew up in Co. Clare and now lives in Boston. Her short stories have appeared in *The Dublin Review*, *The Recorder*, *AGNI*, *The Stinging Fly* and elsewhere.

The dense, warm veil of exhaustion coated Stephen's eyes. Though the window of the car lay half open the billows of night air that buffeted his cheek, his locks, his earlobe did little to revive him. All seemed fuzz, from the steering wheel beneath his hands to the accelerator under his foot. The Alps had witnessed the close of day with him and now they stood over him again on the coming of a new one. In the meantime he had snatched some sleep in a lay-by during the darkest hours of the night. How long he slept he was not sure. Minutes it felt like. All seemed continuation to him, from the sun melting behind the grey peaks beyond Turin last night to the first hint of light this morning. In fact, existence had taken on this zombie-like state for some time before that, ever since he had gotten into the car and started driving two days previously.

With strenuous effort he refocused his eyes that had once again blurred into soft focus on another alpine bend. It was an overcast night that was coming to an end, no stars and only the odd teasing glow of the moon – so different to the night that had seen him embark on this journey.

Then, he had seen nothing like the panorama that presented itself throughout a universe that sought to defy any horizon line. The sky was dense with stars. Now it wasn't worth casting a glance to the sky ahead but that night he laid on his back and tried to breath the cosmos through his eyes. For hundreds of miles in every direction there was no city to cast an electric glow on the heavens. He was on a Greek beach, perched on the opposite edge of Europe. He would sit up. The barbeque let off a warm glow that would struggle to cook the svlakis, burgers and sausages through.

'Shouldn't have gone with the disposable barbeque', Eamon said.

'Well, Jesus, Eamon', Stephen replied, 'there's nothing we can do about it now'. It was clear that there would be slim pickings for the five friends.

'Anyone for another beer?' Frankie chirped in after a moment's silence. So often the intermediary these days, poor Frankie. The three of them, Stephen, Eamon and Frankie, had lived together in a one bedroom apartment for over four months at that stage. Of course tempers would start to fray in that heated and cramped atmosphere, especially given that Stephen and Eamon worked together also. And such strong characters the pair of them were, so similar, Frankie thought. Best friends for years but they'd seen too much of each other this summer and Frankie, poor affable Frankie, was increasingly relied upon to break the tense silences that would descend on them after some niggle or other. In any case, he dispensed another round of beers to the others sitting cross-legged around the barbeque.

Stephen turned a few of the burgers over.

'Have you gotten to know many Greeks over here?' Amy asked before taking another slow drag of the joint.

'Not really', Frankie said, 'maybe just from work, the odd barman down the strip. They keep to themselves mostly'.

'Yeah', continued Eamon, 'for the most part they're content just to take our money, build more Irish bars and bitch about us all the way'.

The sea softly crashed against the rocks below them.

'Really?' said Matt, Amy's boyfriend, 'is it as bad as that?'

'They don't really have a lot of time for us', Frankie replied compromisingly before Eamon could continue. Already a lot of alcohol had been consumed.

The barbeque was in honour of the couple's visit. Matt and Amy were friends from home and were over on a week's holiday. The three lads had known Matt for years and had knocked around with him since the start of secondary school. Since he had started seeing Amy some two years before, they had grown apart slightly as is natural in such cases. However the bitterness that they felt towards the girl in the first few months had passed as she turned out to be a sound character. The glow of the barbeque lit up her brown eyes and Stephen, who had been drinking silently for some time now, thought how lucky Matt had been to find someone like her; someone cool, pretty, laid back. At the start of the summer Stephen rarely thought like this, of regularity, of commitment. But there had been so many sloppy encounters over the summer. Only a few months ago he had been like a kid in a candy shop. So many drunk, easy Irish women, so little time. But now … now, what had seemed like flippant, harmless fun felt more like base animal instincts, sordid, shallow escapades. When had it all changed? It was possible to pinpoint it, he thought. The night with the Kildare girl. Yes, yes that was it. The night in the police station … Stephen felt a chill inside that he tried to thaw by downing his beer and gazing at Amy through the warm glow of the barbeque. A gust of wind caught her loose, light brown hair as she took one final drag of the joint before passing it on to her boyfriend.

'Fuck!' Eamon exclaimed, 'that's nearly blown out half the coals. Should have camped on the beach'.

Stephen fixed his jaw as his meditation on Amy's face had been interrupted by this whiney bastard. The choice had been the shelter and soft sand of the beach or the panorama of the cliff. They had chosen the latter. 'Why must he linger on every little decision that doesn't go his way?' thought Stephen, the spark of his irritation being fanned by alcohol into something approaching anger. The undercurrent of 'I told you so' in Eamon's words suddenly seemed symptomatic, a smug, childish character trait that had grated on Stephen all summer.

'Well, Jesus, Eamon', Stephen said for the second time, 'there's nothing that we can do about it now!'

Eamon smarted at the response this time: 'Well, if you…' he began.

'Shots!' interrupted Frankie.

Poor Frankie. He had already removed the top of the Ouzo bottle. The two friends exchanged a cold look and let it lie. Frankie addressed Matt and Amy; 'Wait till you try this stuff', he said, 'It'll blow your head off'.

Shot glasses were held out and Ouzo was deposited to all five. The potent Greek spirit was taken with gusto but was followed by excruciated faces. They were on their way now.

'I fucking hate the Greeks', Eamon said after a few moments, clearly still holding over some opinions from the previous conversation. 'Nobody pays their taxes, their country is in shit but they still have this attitude towards the Irish. They think we're idiots; 'we build more Irish bars we make meeeeeellions'', he said tailing off into a ridiculous Greek accent.

There were a few chuckles.

'Well I don't know man', Stephen countered, staring blankly into the flames, 'their country can't be in that much shit if they had the Olympic Games last year ...' He looked up with a hint of a challenge in his eyes, '... that's a pretty big deal'.

Matt wondered if Eamon had claimed the opposite would Stephen still have disagreed. Frankie fidgeted.

'Don't get me started on that', Eamon said, 'that's just another case of them living off a two and a half thousand year old reputation. You saw Athens. It's a mess. They got that Olympics off the back of two and a half thousand year old dead people. The Olympics loves romance more than a decent city. When the nicest building in your town was designed and built BC, something has gone horribly wrong'.

Stephen made as if to respond.

'Shots!' Frankie said.

Once again the Ouzo was dispensed.

'Handy enough soccer team, the Greeks', Matt said vaguely.

'None too skilful, but well organised', says Frankie.

'That's another thing', Eamon began again, 'they mightn't have been too bad before, but last year made them unbearable; winning the European Championships and hosting the Olympics in the same year. They've lost a grip on reality for the next hundred years'.

'Don't forget about the Eurovision …' Matt chirped in.

'Yes, don't forget the Eurovision', Eamon laughed, 'talk about delusions of grandeur'.

All laughed – besides Stephen, of course, who seemed growingly irritated that the crowd had turned towards Eamon's opinion. Eamon was aware of this in only the way friends can be. Also, he was more than willing to turn the screw on Stephen, once again, in only the way that close friends can. He decided to go for the deliberate, populist, tabloid-style conclusion that he knew would wreck Stephen's head.

'I mean, about three weeks ago myself and Frankie were getting a taxi home', Eamon addressed the couple; 'and Frankie puked, Godblessim, you know the way Frankie can't handle his drink …'

He sent a wicked, mischievous smile over to Frankie.

'Nothing got on the car, mind, it was all over himself. Barely a drop touched the seat. So the taxi-driver pulls over and is like '€100 NOW!' And I goes 'no way! There's nothing on the car! I'll give you €20'. He goes 'you bloody Irish!' And I'm like 'whataya mean 'you bloody Irish', you mean us bloody Irish that are the sum total of your economy, that put food on your table, that feed your kids!' Eamon concluded smugly, catching Stephen's eye for a microsecond.

It was decided. He was right, the Greeks were wasters. Their country was a mess. Stephen looked coldly across at his friend. He, himself, felt tipsy, but he could tell that Eamon was drunk, more so than the rest of them.

'Maybe the taxi driver was like that', Stephen said, 'because he's had to deal with drunken fuckin' Paddies like you, night in night out. An Irish taxi-driver would have done the same. Smarter people than you and me think we're identical, the Irish and the Greeks. Drinkers, poets and chancers'.

'Whatever', Eamon replied, clearly content that the argument was over. He stood up. 'Pass the spliff, I gotta talk a piss'.

'And who cares if they don't pay their taxes', Stephen continued, clearly unwilling to let the matter lie, 'for how many years did the Irish screw the system in every way possible. How many farmers still screw the system in every possible way, ripping off the Government, thinking it's their due'.

Eamon, who had begun to walk towards the cliff-edge to relieve himself stopped just short, turned and faced the group again. They were only a matter of metres away. It had been a calculated blow. Eamon was of farming stock and fiercely defensive of his heritage, the heritage of his father, long gone.

'Fuck you, Stephen', he said evenly, 'this country is a joke. You know it and I know it'.

The other three watched the exchange between the two friends awkwardly. Frankie felt impotent, it had gone too far now for any flippant comment of his to be able to defuse the situation. Matt remembered Eamon's temper. He waited for an explosion, the overflow of rage that Eamon was known for all those years ago, back when all four lads were close, back when Eamon was an angry and grieving young man. But it didn't happen. Eamon just took a prolonged drag of the joint.

'Ser, even the police', he continued, 'they're a joke. Remember that night you were in the police station. They were watching porn, ser'.

After a moment, Matt allowed himself to breath again. Eamon had let it go. This was a new anecdote, probably just a funny story; drunk and disorderly or something ... maybe dancing on the bonnet of a car just like last time. Matt felt the atmosphere had lightened enough for him to jump in.

'What's all this about a police station?' he said turning to Stephen with a slightly nervous smile. It was at that moment that he realised something was wrong. Stephen's face, whether naturally or by the light of the moon, was paler than normal. Eamon stood defiantly. The others immediately became aware of some line having been crossed, some pact having been broken.

Stephen got up, walked slowly towards his friend. His head was in turmoil. How could Eamon have brought up that night!? That night with the Kildare girl, the night when in the cold, electric light of a sleazy bar bathroom, all of his previous slips came together into one recognisable fall. He had changed. And she so pretty and pale, like porcelain. But she couldn't focus. No, she couldn't focus, eyes roamed around a bit. It didn't feel so good after. And later; the cold steel of the handcuffs on his wrists; the three, moustachioed Greek cops smoking in the room, laughing, watching porn while he was in chaos. The silent, pale figure of that delicate Kildare girl as she blanked him walking unevenly out of the station, swaying slightly. Like a ghost. She was only eighteen and hadn't really objected. They didn't care, the cops in the station. Even the head guy in the office who interviewed him seemed little concerned. A quick in and out. Eamon had stood with him awkwardly outside the station, unsure of what to say. So they simply decided to let it never exist. Never mention it. It was over. It would never get home.

And as Stephen had walked home he felt like he should have been punished. Yet he was so relieved. Fumbling in the bathroom with her, so pale she was. They were both drunk, but him not so much, her especially so. She hadn't really objected. That was her friends afterwards. Then, why did he feel so empty, so rotten? It gnawed and ate away at him. She was so pale. And now … now three oblivious faces looked at him inquiringly, three friends; a couple in love and affable Frankie. Good people. How could he look them in the eye? And his best friend, his conspirator had hung him out to dry, left him dangling in his shame and grief in front of the others. He marched over to Eamon and grabbed him by the neck. He hadn't wanted it to come to this but it was unavoidable now. Too much had been said. The trickle of insults exchanged over the summer had escalated into a stream of sly blows of late, and now, lubricated by alcohol, it had all come to a head. It had to be sorted now. There was no other way for two as close as them. Eamon grabbed his friend's offending wrist with one hand and clutched his jersey with his other hand, pulling Stephen closer. For just one moment the two glared into each other's eyes, within a hair's breadth. They stood silhouetted against the canvas of the night sky, light of a million stars arriving late, as clear to them then in that place as it was to Plato and Aristotle before. And for that moment Matt, Amy and Frankie thought that it wouldn't go any further than this, a quick intense grapple to burn off the testorone. But it did go further.

'Ah lads!' Frankie said, getting up quickly. Matt too, got up and approached the grappling, punching couple. Amy looked horrified but too stoned, slow and confused to move. Stephen now managed to get Eamon's head down into a headlock, whose bucking and frantic blows sent the pair rocking erratically, at times moving perilously close to the cliff-edge. Stephen grunted as he attempted to keep his friends flailing body under control, his neck locked between his bicep and forearm. 'It's too dangerous now', thought Matt who normally would have let the two get it out of their system.

'C'mon lads', he said, 'we've all had a bit to drink', and he tried to loosen Stephen's grip on his friend.

A big lad was Matt and he was having success. Frankie though, so gawky and weak, had locked his bony arms under Stephen's armpits. He was trying to pull him the opposite direction. Stephen raged against the restraining force but he was getting tired. He couldn't hold the headlock any longer. Matt's cold, firm grip levered his arms apart. Frankie still tugged irritatingly off him. And as the two fighters were wrenched apart Eamon gave one final kick, catching Stephen on the shin. Before he could react, Matt stood between them. All were breathing heavily. It was the only noise but for the slow crashing of the waves below them. The fighters stared at each other. They stood a moment away from normality. The stark descent of the ego was not far off; that microsecond when the mist of fury clears and one is faced with a ludicrous situation. They would see themselves, panting on a moonlit cliff-edge, base creatures acting out base instincts. But that moment hadn't quite been reached.

'C'mon', Frankie said, and tried to pull Stephen away. And suddenly all of Stephen's fury was directed at this figure pulling off him.

'Will you fuck off!' he roared and pivoted and shoved Frankie.

Then things started happening slowly. The weaker man stumbled backwards, catching Stephen's eye for a moment. 'He looks confused', Stephen thought as the inexorable pull of momentum and gravity carried Frankie's body backwards. The parched Greek earth of the cliff-edge, baked for half a year, did not last long beneath the foot of the Irishman. It crumbled and slid into the blackness – as did Frankie, still looking confused, toppling backwards into the night.

And now, two days later, it was that darkness that Stephen saw when he rested his eyes for a moment. It was getting harder and harder to open them again though. The light was getting brighter and the road markings blurred and hurt his head. The darkness was pure comfort. Sometimes though, Frankie's confused face would flash across his mind's eye. He couldn't clasp his hand, not in a mere moment of shut-eye. As the sun slid up above the Alps behind him he felt no affinity for the day, for the waking world, for the road ahead of him. The light hurt his eyes. He needed to stay in the dark that bit longer. For Frankie; long enough to grab him this time. The hum of the car around him, he looked at the road ahead one last time. It was bright now. He slipped into darkness. Pure comfort. He would have to stay longer this time. For Frankie.

E.P. de Búrca is a Limerick-based writer and poet. As a student of languages, he spent recent years living between Spain, Greece and the USA. He is involved in journalism and contributes regular pieces to various local publications.

NUALA NI CHONCHUIR

Toys

I was given the dead girl's toys: a blonde baby-doll with sheeny limbs and pen-mark squiggles on her rubber belly; some story books; a homemade dolly-cradle with crocheted blankets; an apple-red train engine, and a squat stuffed horse that had a corduroy coat. Her father came to our house with the toys one afternoon, a few weeks after the funeral. When my mother saw through the door-glass that it was him, she cursed quietly, took off her apron and ran her hands over her hair. I stood behind her in the hall.

'Matthew'. She held the front-door wide. 'Come in'.

'I won't, Belle. I just wanted to give you these', he held up a cardboard box with toys in it. 'For your daughter. We wanted them out of the house'.

His jacket had a slide of gravy down the front and his face was dirty with a young beard. He handed the box to my mother and looked straight at her; she took it, left it down and stepped out into the porch. I inched towards the box and my mother flicked her fingers at me to keep me away. They stood close, facing each other, their eyes down.

'I'm so sorry, Matthew …' My mother moved her hand forward, then withdrew it.

He nodded, whispered, 'I know, Belle', and backed away from her, down our driveway.

I had never heard anyone call my mother Belle before – everyone we knew called her Isabelle or Izzy. I hadn't known that she knew the dead girl's family, either. She'd never said.

My mother read to me that night, as usual. She tuckled under my blankets with me, all her clothes still on and her feet snug in fleshy tights. The box of toys lurked by the wardrobe in the corner of my room; I had poked through them and thought my own toys were much better. I could hear the television's thrum from the sitting-room below; my father sat there by himself, half-reading the paper, half-watching a programme. When she'd finished reading stories, my mother tamped down my hair with her fingers and asked me if I knew that she loved me very much.

'Yes, I *do* know that you love me very much', I said, twisting my fingers into hers and cuddling into her side. 'And I love *you* very much, Belle'.

'Don't say that'. She dropped my hand and swung out of the bed; her face creased up. 'Don't call me that again'. She waggled her finger at me.

'OK, Mam'. I was sorry I had annoyed her. 'Kiss?'

My mother sighed, 'Kiss'. She put her hands over my cheeks and kissed my forehead. 'Good night, love'.

The dead girl had gone missing on the way home from school on a bright Monday afternoon; her body was found the following Friday, in the woods at the end of the town. Our parents closed in on us during that time, they watched every move we made. In the five days she was missing, her name – Martha Sweeney – was in every newspaper and on the television each night. It was all we talked about at school. The teachers made a shrine to Martha on a low table in the school hallway. The photo from the paper was put in a frame; it was flanked by two candles and a tea-glass filled with carnation buds. Martha was ten – two years older than me – and I wasn't really sure if I'd ever noticed her around the school. But after a while, from the photo that was everywhere, her face was as familiar to me as my own: I knew the crease of her smile, her large eyebrows, the floppy black fringe. Somebody said I looked a bit like her.

The day Martha was found, the teachers assembled the whole school in the hallway at morning break.

'I have very sad news for you, girls', the principal said, bowing her head. 'Little Martha Sweeney's body was found this morning'.

I remember it took me a minute to realise that what the principal meant was that Martha was dead; I stared up at her, then around at everyone else. Some girls began to cry. We all stood in front of the table-shrine, held hands, and said prayers.

'Oh, Angel of God, my guardian dear', we chanted, 'to whom God's love commits me here, ever this day be at my side, to light, to guard, to rule and guide. Amen'.

After praying, we all stood around in groups, whispering, not knowing what to do next.

'I bet she was half-naked when they found her', one of the older girls said to a gaggle of us littler ones.

'She was probably strangled with a man's tie', her friend said, staring around at us.

'Or a belt'. We gasped and held our throats.

'She knew him, I'd say, whoever he was. That's the usual thing'.

Then the two big girls shored-up their lips, rolled eyes at each other, and walked away. I stood with my friends and we said nothing.

I looked over at the huddle of teachers; they seemed different with tears on their faces, I thought – more like real people. We were sent home early and, like every other day that week, and for a time afterwards, our mothers were waiting to meet us at the school-gates, to take us straight home.

It was probably a month or so after he'd come to the door with the box of toys, that I saw Mr Sweeney again. My mother had stopped collecting me after school every day and I was free to dawdle home, the way I used to. I had stopped in front of the sweetshop and was breathing in the mushroomy smell from the doorway, trying to decide what goodies to buy, when he walked up and stood beside me.

'Hello', he said.

I looked up at him; his dark hair was grease-heavy and his clothes were mussed up.

'Hello'.

'How is your Mammy?'

I jiggled my feet and hefted my schoolbag forward on my shoulders. 'She's grand'.

'Good, good'. He scratched his face. 'And how are you?' He bent nearer to me; his breath was sour, like old tea.

'I'm fine'. I turned away. 'I have to go now'.

I ducked into the shop; Mr Sweeney stayed outside for a minute, looking through the window at me, then he walked off. I didn't tell my mother that I'd met him.

He started to follow me after that; I'd see him most days, lurching his car along beside the pathway as I walked home. Sometimes he'd walk behind me, all the way from the school to my house. I would stop suddenly, so that he'd have to stop too, and it became a little game we played: me letting him know that I knew he was behind me all the time. I didn't think to be afraid of him – my mother had invited him into our house that time when he'd come with the box of toys. He was someone we knew.

At home, I started to play with Martha's toys: I put the baby-doll into a white sleep-suit belonging to one of my own dolls and lay her down in the cradle, under her coloured blankets. I sang to her: 'Hush little Minnie and don't say a word, Papa's gonna buy you a mocking-bird', and patted her plastic cheek. I read to her from Martha's story-books; I sat her up on the corduroy horse and pretended she was a cow-girl, yeee-haaah. Then I whizzed her up and down the hall in the red train engine.

'You're getting a bit big for dollies aren't you, pet?' my mother said, frowning at me from the kitchen doorway.

'No'. I careened the baby-doll back up the hallway in her train and glared at my mother.

'Well, maybe we should clear out some of those old things…those old toys'.

I grabbed the doll and the engine and marched away from her, up the stairs to my room.

'Hello again'.

Mr Sweeney had parked his car at the end of our road and he wound down the window to talk to me.

'Hello'. I smiled, swinging my skipping-rope in one hand.

'That's a lovely dress you're wearing'.

'Thank you, it's new'.

I ran my fingers over the skirt of my blue dress; my mother had made it for me. It was Sunday and we were going to visit my cousins on the other side of town. Mr Sweeney clicked open his car door and stood out on to the path. His eyes were wide open and stary, and he kept swallowing as if he was about to say something. He put his hand out to me but I didn't want to touch it.

'Martha', he said. I inched backwards towards our driveway. 'Martha'.

He started to shake all up and down his body, then he lunged forward and fell against me, knocking me off my feet. My side and arm hit off the cement path and Mr Sweeney lay across me, hugging me, rocking me in his arms and saying, 'Martha, Martha, Martha', into my hair. I wriggled and pushed, trying to get him off me.

'Stop, stop'. I could hardly hear my own screams.

'Matthew, Matthew', my mother's voice flew around my ears and I felt myself being pulled up off the ground, the backs of my legs scraping on pebbles. My father lifted me into my mother's arms. He stood over Mr Sweeney who was kneeling by now on the path, sobbing.

'Stay away from my family, do you hear me, Sweeney? Do you hear me?' My father pushed him and Mr Sweeney sagged forward. Then he dragged himself up. He stood in front of us and tried to speak but nothing came out. He turned away, walked to his car and slumped into the driver's seat, his face torn. He drove off without looking at us. My mother held me close and kissed my cheeks; she kept asking me if I was OK and I said that I was. I watched the car drive away. 'Bloody fool', my father said and guided my mother and me indoors.

I was put to bed, though it was early afternoon, and I lay there, listening to my parents argue downstairs, until I fell away into sleep. Nobody was ever caught for killing Martha and I didn't see Mr Sweeney again after that.

Nuala Ní Chonchúir lives in Loughrea, Co. Galway. Her first collection of short stories, *The Wind Across the Grass*, was published in 2004 by Arlen House; her second collection, *To the World of Men, Welcome*, was launched in March 2006. She is the recipient of numerous prizes for her fiction, including the Francis MacManus Award (2002), the Cecil Day Lewis Award (2003) and the inaugural Cúirt New Writing Prize (2004). Her first poetry collection, *Molly's Daughter* was published in volume one of the Arlen House *DIVAS!* series and she edited Volume 2 entitled *DIVAS!: A Sense of Place* which is an anthology of 50 Galway women writers (Arlen House, 2005).

ZOE WICOMB

An Excerpt from *Playing in the Light*

It was still dark, still night, with the dense blackness that you did not get in town, where streetlight turned the night sky to a murky brown. John turned on the lumpy horsehair mattress to check the time, and the iron bedstead creaked; he looked anxiously across the room to where the child slept. She swallowed and muttered. In the dark he thought he could see the glow of her pale face, her golden hair: Marion, his darling mermaid. In the kitchen he heard the shuffling of his mother's feet on the linoleum, the sound of pots and pans. It was five o'clock. He crept out of bed, took the bundle of clothes and shoes, and dressed in the narrow passage.

The stove was already lit, logs glowing red in the lamplight, and the coffee beans in the pan were just beginning to discolour, releasing the aroma of his own childhood – so that when Ma came out of the pantry to give the pan a shake, he would have liked to bury his head in her aproned bosom. Instead, he said that it was early, that it was still darkest night outside.

Ag no my child, listen to the finches out in the willows – they've been busy for hours, their families already fed, and here I am still roasting the coffee.

In town, he said, the sky is brownish, never fully black.

Well, that's a pity. You won't be able to see the stars properly then.

No, he said, not much of a show of stars.

The truth was that he hadn't really thought about stars. What kind of boer was he, he chided himself, who didn't care about the night sky, who slipped so effortlessly into city life? Of course he belonged to this land, to the farm, and the next morning he would be out there with Pa, milking the cows, setting the cabbage seedlings. Now that they'd all left to make their livings elsewhere, his father had hired a boy from Bergplaas; but John should have remembered how much there was to do, should already have been out there on the land like a proper farmer.

One of these days I must come to town, said Ma, come and see how you people live there without stars. It's a disgrace that I've had to wait so long to see my own grandchild, and who knows when I'll see her next. That Helen of yours will think of some excuse why she can't come on the train with you. I don't know what's come over Helen – such a nice girl, shy and modest she was when you first brought her, but now so full of airs and graces, as if we're not good enough.

Ma-aa, he remonstrated feebly. There was nothing to say in defence of Helen.

Perhaps in the autumn, the old woman said, after the harvest, I'll come to town. But I don't like the train, you know; I'm too spoilt by the horses that do as they're told.

She was sitting with her legs astride, the coffee grinder on her lap; an old woman with painterly wrinkles, her right hand grinding with effort and her slanted eyes following the hand abstractedly, as if she'd forgotten that he was there.

Through the whirr of the grinder he said, Ma, you must come. You'd love a little holiday in town – have coffee brought to you in bed for a change.

John spoke from the heart. He meant every word, although he knew that she could not come to stay with him. But then, his mother would not really have been able to leave the farm, would in any case have found an excuse not to come. He would get another bed put into Marion's room, where Ma could have a lie-in. Early in the morning, at five, because she was sure to be awake at that time, before Helen woke, he'd bring her coffee; he'd shut the door, and the three of them would sip coffee and dunk their rusks in that room sealed from the city and its devilish complications. For that was now city life, full of complications; but he had no trouble envisioning the impossible, substituting the cosy image of familial harmony. His heart lightened at the promise of such a visit.

So that Ma's next question pierced his heart. He did not even recognise that clipped dark voice, the angry eyes lifted from the grinder. Yes, Johnnie, so many of my children now in town, but what about you, hey? You are the eldest, their ouboeta; you should be keeping an eye on them. They are your blood brothers, your only sussie; your house should be the family home away from home.

He squirmed. Ag no Ma, don't spoil things now; Ma knows what a business it is there in town. Of course I see them all. Elsie will tell you how I drop in for Sunday lunch; she phones to say when the others are coming. Sussie Els is such a good cook, it's just like being here at Ma's table, and then we sit lekker together talking about the old days here on the farm. And she sometimes drops in at our house of an evening, she used to; she gets on quite well with Helen. You should see our Els – she is now a bliksem of a driver, just scoots all over town in that black Ford of theirs.

The old woman smiled briefly at his account of Elsie, who had married so well. If she'd ever had reservations about Fourie, they were quite dispelled by the image of her girl being so comfortable, so modern. But she shook her head as she put the cups of coffee and the plate of butter biscuits on the tray and said, My boy, I understand. These things may be necessary and God is good to his children and stepchildren alike, but it's a sin, the whole business is a sin. She looked at him anxiously. It is not enough to have money clinking in your pockets. You must go to church every Sunday, ask God's forgiveness, that's all we can do. So far God has been good to you, giving you this lovely little girl with golden hair, but you must be careful Johnnie, careful to keep an eye on your own flesh and blood.

He wanted to put his arms around her, to reassure her that things were not like that at all, that the world was changing, that life in the city made no such impossible demands of blood relatives. That bettering yourself, taking opportunity by the horns in a country where rules and regulations whizzed like so many darts about your head, could not be such a sinful thing. That the God of the city was not the demanding God of the farm. But she would not understand that, would not want to be hugged, had saved the softness of bodily contact for her grandchildren; she would not accept that human relations, or the demands of blood, could be different in the city.

When Pa came in for breakfast, he tossed the little girl on his knee. Marion squealed with delight, Again Pappa, more horsie-horsie! The old man fondled her golden hair, called her a demanding klein-nooi, and promised her a ride on a real horse the next day. Later, John took her up the ladder to the loft, where he turned the drying apricots and checked the biltong. Marion turned up her nose. It smells like the bubbie's shop, she said. She did not want to touch the strips of drying meat. These things were nothing; the dangerous trip up the ladder was no longer so exciting. Who cared about a loft with a black door high on the side of the house, when tomorrow she and Pappa would fly through the land on horseback, on a real horse? She no longer wanted to be a mermaid; she wanted to be a horse. Could she not be a sea horse?

In the doorway of the loft they sat with their feet on the first rung of the ladder and surveyed the world. They could see the river lined with willows trailing their fingertips in the shallow water, and the proud weaverbirds darting in and out of their show homes. Which Marion, starting fearlessly down the ladder, had to visit right away. Now she was a bird darting hither and thither in a world without boundaries; she would fly off to the river. Ouma marvelled at her energy, at her belief that she could do as she pleased, be anything at all she fancied.

So that, said the old woman, forgetting her own indulgence of the child, that is what it's like being brought up as a klein-nooi.

John no longer minded that Helen could not take her holiday with them. He'd wanted to present Ma with a family, but now, suspecting that Helen did not want to come home to the farm, he was glad that they were on their own. It wasn't loyal, but without her he felt a loosening of his shoulders; here he could be himself, as they said, although he was not entirely sure what that meant. At least he was not responsible for the city traffic; he had a fond idea that the city would snarl up without his guidance – an image that developed into stationary motorists and pedestrians, all promiscuously tangled.

The child lay on her stomach, muttering to herself and trailing her right hand in the water. She'd found a clump of maidenhair fern with leaves of palest green, its partially exposed roots on the very edge of the riverbank, rooted in both earth and water. She held her dripping fingers aloft. Tears dripped from her fingers on to the leaves, so that the fern trembled from its watery roots, and with her left hand she gathered the leaves together like a bunch of garden carrots. Hush little baby, she crooned, don't you cry. Poor, poor little fern, hush for mummy; everything will be alright.

Had she heard them talking last night? Pa's tired, defeated voice: The Boere want the farm, John. It's the river – they want the water.

Ag no Pa, he'd said, everything will be alright; they won't, they just can't. You've been here so long, you've turned this piece of veld into land, into a farm; no, you mustn't worry.

His throat had tightened, stricken with panic, as he uttered the *they* who couldn't, who wouldn't. The Campbells were the ones who farmed this land, small as it was. They too were farmers, boere.

His father had looked at him with incredulity. No? Well, I'm just waiting for the papers. It will be no more than a year before the area is reclassified. You forget, the land belongs to old Serfontein, and he may not be happy about this business, but what can he do? The law is the law. We'll have to try for an erf in the Bergplaas area.

Bergplaas, John repeated in a thin voice. Bergplaas was just not a possibility, not amongst those raggedy Hotnos. It was a stunning thought. His little golden girl could not be exposed to that. What on earth would he do?

God will guide us, his mother had said, resignedly. Bergplaas is not such a terrible place.

John had no quibble with God; he was as obedient, as fearful of God as the next man. But no, much as being home suffused him with guilt, he knew then with certainty that he'd taken the right course. Bergplaas, all higgledy-piggledy smallholdings, was really no more than allotments farmed by defeated coloureds – never on your nelly. He, John Campbell, would never be bullied like that by the law; and as for his child, his little mermaid, she would hold the world in the palm of her pretty hand.

Can I take it home, Pappie? she asked.

He started. No, no – what, the fern? Whatever will you do with it? It would rather be living here in the shade, sipping at the water.

But look, she said, worrying it like a loose milk tooth, it's crying, it doesn't want to go to Bergplaas, and I want to look after it. Then it will grow into the long hair of a mermaid.

So she tugged, and indeed the roots had lost heart and came up with an easy sound of suction. Back at the house, he helped her plant the maidenhair fern in a pot, an old milk pail painted red, that they found on the stoep and from which he shook the dusty corpse of another plant in order to make way for the new one. Ouma will look after it, Marion said.

Patting the child's head abstractedly, the old woman sighed, thinking how her chores seemed to multiply each day, how the smallest task had become such a burden. Already she saw in the fresh greenness of the fern the dried brown skeleton of each frond.

On the train home, John unpacked Ma's basket of fried chicken, ostrich biltong studded with coriander and heavy wheat bread for the overnight train journey.

I've written to Paul. He's at the police station in Mossel Bay, so smart in his uniform, Ma had said proudly. The train arrives at about eleven at night and stops for half an hour, so Paul will be there to see you. She packed a separate bag of biltong and biscuits for John to deliver to her fourth son.

He hadn't seen Paul for a couple of years; he chuckled fondly. Marion, tired of exploring once again the scaled-down, counterfeit world of the coupé – the wooden panelling that concealed a bed of green leather upholstery; the table unmasked to reveal a shiny little stainless-steel sink and a mirror in which to admire herself – was asleep. Which was a pity, since Paul would so love to see her, would be charmed by her pretty klein-nooi speech. Paul would sit with them in their coupé, sipping Ma's coffee from the flask. They were so lucky to have a compartment to themselves. A coupé is nice and private, Helen had said, having made the reservation herself. Although he felt that it took the joy out of travelling if you didn't meet people, share in their outsiders' delight at the sweetness of the child. He liked a good old chat, and people would tell you all kinds of wonderful things about the world, about themselves – especially the new kind of people he met nowadays. Oh, it would be wonderful to see Paul, tall, dark and so handsome; full of jokes and rough talk, but with a heart of gold, oh yes. John's eyes pricked at the thought of seeing his boe-tie.

It was not until the train puffed its way over the mountain and through George, and the lights across the bay winked feebly, that panic set in. How would Paul find him in that section of the train? John thought of Ma's pride in the constable's uniform, khaki like everyone else's, but for all he knew Paul might even be the railway constable, patrolling the coloured platform, in which case he just didn't know how they would manage. Would he have to lean out of the window and somehow hail Paul at the far end of the platform?

The squeal of the rails as the train puffed into the station tore through his heart; the acrid smell of coal and hissing steam were rough, squeezing hands around his throat. John pulled down the blind and switched off the light.

In the morning he gave the sullen bedding boy a bag of biltong and home-made biscuits.

Zoe Wicomb was born in South Africa and currently lives in Glasgow, where she teaches in the University of Strathclyde. Her novel, *David's Story*, which won the South African M-Net Prize, was described by J.M. Coetzee as 'a tremendous achievement and a huge step in the remaking of the South African novel'. This extract is taken from her forthcoming novel, *Playing in the Light*, which will be published by Umuzi/Random House in summer 2006.

Late Night Coffee Bar: 28th March 2004

Saturday night into Sunday morning. Near close. Twenty minutes give or take. Calls for last coffees. Final detonations of sulphur. Chastening whorls of smoke.

Tonight, endangered species abound. Soon-to-be hard-to-find sorts. They have shunned all announcements; hidden from its arrival; fabricated forgotten ideals. They feel gypped. Cut loose. Unacknowledged in the scheme of things. At your peril you mention it. Hairs bristle. Lips bloat and curl. Daggers spool from suddenly lustrous eyes. If you must talk of it cover your mouth; elbow and wink; whisper the little word. This soft café light is no place now or ever for these struck-off amber glints.

Hear their mild rebellions. *Say it isn't true.* Their wistful pleas. *Where will we go?* Talk of their lot to be. *Things just won't be the same.*

Chiselling declamations from a talky kind of singer don't help this end-is-nigh mood. His long throaty lines jostle for a hitch in the smoke-turning room. Piano trickles along. Muted trumpet braves the singer's forlorn gist. Like a clapped-out elephant alone in the bush desert night. And the voice seeps unrelenting through the smoky vibe and unfurling layers of imperceptible static.

Amidst these woe-begun moments here I am. Taking a sip. Stealing my moment.

Unlikely suspirations one and all.

Our waitress prepares herself; folds an apron; eyes the clock. Almost there. Nearly done. The unflappable second hand does its bit. But the vital sign labours. At odds with her onwards yearning, it teases out the closing moment. Prolonging the end with a faltering rhythm. Is it a trick of the light? A test of her wavering dedication? Has this rueful band of smokers cast a spell? A charlatan aspect that possesses the minute hand. Haltingly to the hour mark. Only then can she flee.

Forget about it. Steal those restless eyes elsewhere. Wash some cups. Clear another table. Bequeath a refill to your favourites. You might never see them again.

A shot for the balcony-eyed sergeant alone in the corner. What will his trembling yellow fingers do? He's on duty tonight. The graveyard shift. Hanging out in the quiet side before the move up town. Before silly time. And he must push himself between six-day-fasting-frenzied youths trying to rip one another's heart out. To uphold a blood soaked prestige. And the pride of a ramshackle cause.

Two steaming mugs for a grouty pair beneath the bookshelf wall. Company for the pouch of Golden Virginia and Rizla rolls they work with meticulous zest. Super-sizing to mark the occasion.

A glass with a handle for the slip-of-a-thing at the window. On a high stool. Right next to me. Hidden for the most part behind the steadily turning pages of a graphic novel. In between deft flicks of a done-and-dusted page her cigarette arm protrudes like an elegant spout. And busy eyes scroll up and down the intricate designs of the picture tale. Its title is concealed, like a hologram, within the outstretched arms of a green-bandage cadaver that walks towards a frothing ghoul rising from the bubbling muds. Bleeding black letters on the back cover spell out instantaneous perils of forgoing next month's issue.

At the table below me three wanderers. Two guys and a girl. Backpacks that have brought the elephant to its knees. Stitched on revelations. *Cats have got nine lives but you've only got one. I love to travel, but hate to arrive. In the potholes is where it's at.* Between artificial puffs of a leaded pencil, the girl bladders like there's no tomorrow. She could talk for her country and soon makes the discovery. 'I'm a very oral person', she announces and, dragging heavily on her pencil, a tacked-on corollary spells it out a little more: 'I always have to have something in my mouth'.

She launches a tablet of gum, lays down the pencil, tilts her head and traps the returning pill between her teeth. Then gnashes into her prize.

Abetted by a folding map, the other two plot a way out.

As a boy I harboured dreams of travel. I turned atlas pages. Memorised capital cities. Pined for strange horizons. Paramaribo. Gantok. Ouagadougou. Geography was my subject. Each moment became a lesson. Every game revealed my wish. I wanted to hike across a continent. Say hi in every language. Become infatuated with a sallow skinned girl. It was all very exotic. I made secret promises. Immersed myself in complicated sagas. Tried to giddyup the time. And when it came I couldn't move.

Over the bookshelf monochrome mounts depict cities by night. Three dark-towns of gloom. Cityscapes oozing rue. In spite of it all the bookshelf sags into a smile, invading the space between the Rizla rollers, low-down in confidential bidding. The plot unfurls beneath the brooding city nights. A pantomime straight from the silver screen. Wise guy and flunkey. The brains of the intrigue. And the no-brains. Either side of a tinny ashtray. Rollies burning down.

Brains is busy. An index finger points to his ear and performs tiny orbits. While his other hand curls into a fist. And a torqued forearm follows through. As though someone must thrust well with a blade. What are they hatching? A weighty deed for the flunkey. A stand to the last ditch. The beginning of mad things.

Beneath a Chinese hat, a pair of rippling jowls presses against the window. The owner wobbles in; allows the hat fall back at his neck; where it's held by a string.

He's had a few but carries it well. A content-looking man. Recently retired perhaps. His health is rude. And people in his family live a long time. Maybe he just got out of the clink. Straight to the till with him. And to the waitress: 'I'd like a large pint of Guinness please'. Soft. Patient. Knowing. A poker face to bring down the house and a mien no girl wants to disappoint. A devil of a performer. 'Wait', she says indulging for the moment the impish whim. And she disappears out back.

I used to drink in a bar at the end of this road. Along the narrow street; down an alley; a sawdust floor and cut-out keg pews. Low tables by the wall. A candle for the dim light. I used to bring a girl there. We talked about it all; forgot the time; drank the rent. We shielded our eyes when we left, skipped down to the pier and fed the swans. We tiptoed home across the bridge; told each other we'd stay awake forever and fell asleep to the sounds of clattering beer crates. When they shut it down I got drunk and said I'd open it again. It was something I really wanted to believe. A reluctance to let go. And the romance of the unattainable.

Thereabouts, nowadays, a flurry of casino-neon lights up another fancy and the beefy doorman stands over the pot of gold. As for the girl ◎◎she won the lotto, packed her bags and ruined her dainty feet. At least that's what she tells me happens in her dreams.

No-brains stares at the talking head opposite him. All the time. In awe. As though it is full of wonders he lacks. Gusto and spleen. Attitude and can-do. Brains knows this. He oozes wisdom and his effervescence compels. Ferociously, he wags the pointing finger in his cohort's face. Conferring the plot's true essence. While sparring with a tortuous learner. No-brains hangs off every word, gesture and vibe. He wears an army green brim hat ringed with a felt blue mantra *I am a fucking paddy.* Metallic figurines dangle from the hat. A walking boot; a pistol; a loaded dice; and a long roofless car with fins. Vigorously, he nods his head at the wagging finger. Grateful to be a part in the deed. Inside the circle. Part of the shakedown. Meanwhile the figurines tremble. Like death-watches. In the sticks of a kindling flame. Because they know.

A metal hiss floods the low-key room. Mucky spume sloshes through a rib-neck glass. The drinker ducks beneath his triangular crown. Caresses settle time along. Like a child at Christmas time. In thrall to the unexpected gift.

He lets our waitress in on his ruse.

'I don't know', she replies. 'A little ghost out back tells me you're a serious-in-jest kind of guy'.

'It is a good-looking drink'.

'I've heard tell it can put a chest on a man's hairs'.

'I don't suppose you've any onions'.

'My God, an onion eater to boot'.

'The breath drives the missus doo-lally'.

'I'm sure she wouldn't have you any other way'.

'She can be a force of nature'.

'And you're a terrible man. In cahoots with the wee hours of the night'.

'Do you like my hat?'

'That hat is definitely wrong'.

But he leaves it on anyway.

I have a four-year-old nephew who calls me Mr. Wrong. I can't remember how it started. He drew a picture of a house with crooked walls and oblong windows and an upside down door. The garden was full of weeds. The chimney was on fire. He said it was where I lived. He even drew a Mrs. Wrong – a stick insect with feet growing out of her head. She was in the kitchen tucking into the instructions for a Zanussi. I'm going to use him for bait the next time I go to the lake. Or maybe put him in a room with the terrible frog.

A guy with a sleeved guitar appears. The girl's eyes smile.

'What's happening?' he says mimicking a fiend from her gory story.

But she is rescued by the chiming register. And the jingling coin basket. And the spluttering coffee machine that appears to have run out of steam.

Our waitress kills the music; draws the catch; holds the door.

And it occurs to everyone: The minute hand has fallen into place.

The wanderers swing their packs towards the night, the sergeant already gone.

The large-pint-of-muck man doffs his hat; mulls over a gesture; and crowns his latest queen.

No-brains looks to Brains for a way to fend off the inevitable.

Two o'clock and ticking. Been a long day. Waitress wants home. To dress down. Unwind. Without sermon, she turfs us out. But I don't mind. Time to move on. Face the world. Make some new mistakes. Contrive a misunderstanding. Hesitate. Speak at the bad time.

Which is why sometimes, once every now and again; on the occasion of a blue moon; at the unreasonable hour; in the time it takes to smoke one final cigarette; as the elephant's lonely trumpet seeks his ancestor's trail and the wanderer's soliloquy scatters through the vast valley silence, and the lines of the low tunes ripple slowly through the room like the spreading rings about a raindrop that touches the unmoving water, and silent epiphanies rush the seconds in between songs, and I really haven't very much to say, this is where I like to be. The other side of midnight. Saturday night into Sunday morning. At the quiet end. Where the meter doesn't tick as fast. When solace reigns and ghosts oblige. For twenty minutes. Or thereabouts. Before closing time.

I can taste the ocean now. The blue moon begins to turn again. Tonight, I think I'll walk home to my crooked house; stir my good lady from her wealthy dreams; sort out her crumpled feet; ask her what she wants to see; lace some walking boots; comment on the waning solstice; and tell her let's go.

Alan McMonagle lives in Galway. To date his work has appeared in *Galway Now*, *Virtual Writer* and he was recently shortlisted in the *Bibliofemme* fiction competition. He is also a regular contributor to the UK travel publication *Outdoor Adventure*. He is currently working on his first collection of stories.

CRISTINA CONA

The Devil's Daughter

Year after year, on the eve of January the sixth she would hang her stocking up outside the farm door. The Befana, the old woman who brought gifts to all good children, would no doubt call during the night and leave something for her. But early the next morning, when she tiptoed downstairs and peeped outside, the stocking would be empty, frozen into flat cardboard stiffness by the icy cold. 'I must be really wicked, so', she'd think.

As the years went by, of course, she would first suspect and then fully take in that the reason for the empty stockings had been her parents' meanness, their inability to think in terms other than of saving money. Not all her relatives were like that. Her aunt Carulin, who wasn't any richer than they were, still managed to give her family something special for Christmas. She'd bake a bun, roughly shaped like a baby, and tie a pale blue ribbon round its waist when she took it out of the oven. 'Look, children', she'd say, 'the baby Jesus was in the oven but the ribbon didn't burn. Isn't that a miracle?'

For her own parents, there were no such things as miracles. You worked hard, you saved, you lived on the bare minimum. She was lucky though. There were families around them who even kept their children short of bread. At least in her own house they could eat as much bread as they liked. Not that there was much else. Polenta and soup every day, occasionally an egg. Before setting off for school they ate dinner leftovers – the slices of polenta roasted on the fire, the thick soup fried. None of the newfangled foods sold at the market ever made it to their house. Her mother said chocolate was cat shit.

Any fun had to be snatched from life and fought for. She'd skip school when the travelling fair came to the town, in order to see the man with the dancing bears. Afterwards she'd scribble a note for the nuns – 'She has stayed at home for family use'. Her parents were illiterate, and the nuns knew it, but they were probably glad to have been given a break even for one day. She was rebellious, contrary, sharp-tongued. She was always teasing the teachers and bullying the other pupils. She refused to accept that the Pope was infallible. 'He's just an ordinary man', she'd say. Once the class had been taken to a nearby village on a day trip, a rare treat which had involved getting up at dawn and walking for hours under the scorching sun. There was a small Protestant community in that village, and the girls had been forbidden to enter the heretical church. Mortal sin, the nuns had said. Of course she'd sneaked in and had a good look, disappointed because among those pictureless, statueless walls there hadn't been much to see.

Another treat was tormenting people – throwing the small thistle heads they called 'cicapui', those spiky things that clung inextricably to wool and hair, into the braided tresses of women so that it would take them hours to undo the mess, their eyes brimming with indignant tears; she beat up other children. Boys would scatter when they saw her coming. She'd defend her sister, who was five years older and totally incapable of fighting, against fellows her sister's age. When threatened with punishment she'd run away, climb trees, stay up there among the branches until the sun came down and even her father got tired of waiting with a stick in his hand.

And then there was the milk she stole from the well, and there were the dead bodies. The milk she'd drink from the bucket which her parents had left in the well to cool. All the milk in the house was for sale. She'd sneak up to the well, hoist the bucket up from the depths, slurp down all that thick, creamy froth she was not supposed to taste.

The dead. Whenever she heard that someone had died she'd go to the house, whether or not she knew the people. She'd mingle with the crowd who'd come to pay their respects, enter the room where the body was laid out and just look and look, take in every detail, fascinated. She just couldn't understand those women who were too squeamish to wash and dress corpses. But then, some women were like that, soft and sentimental, no stamina, no devilry inside them. Doormats.

Like her sister. Francesca was a real beauty, blue-eyed and fair-haired, and one of those people who wouldn't hurt a fly – couldn't catch one, most likely. She had expressed a desire to become a nun, but the parents wouldn't hear of it. Novices were requested to bring in their own linen, which would be kept by the convent if the girl eventually decided not to take the vows. What if Francesca changed her mind? The family would lose all that good stuff, all those sheets and towels, gone to waste, left with the nuns. All that money down the drain. No, it couldn't be.

So they got her a husband. Giuseppe was ten years older than her, a beekeeper and farmer of genius; he had devised a way of ensuring that the apples stored in the pantry would stay fresh and edible all winter, by injecting some substance into them while they were still in bud. He was also paranoid about cleanliness, and carried a bottle of methylated spirits on him so that he could disinfect all household objects, as well as his own hands, as soon as other people had touched them. And he was a very religious man. He had been a good accordion player in his youth, but one day he had been scolded by the parish priest for playing dance music and leading young people into temptation and sin. He had gone home, taken off the accordion, hung it on the wall, and never played it again.

So religious – that was a very good thing, her mother said. So chaste, he had never touched a woman in his life. When they came back from their honeymoon they were both still virgins because he had no idea how to do it. He went to the priest for advice. The priest explained it all to him, and added, 'You must always sow in the field, never outside it'. The Church had spoken, he obeyed, and spent the next few years impregnating his wife. So many children, three girls and one boy, in nonstop succession, until Francesca's body gave up.

She got tuberculosis while pregnant for the fifth time and died very quickly, exhausted as she'd been for a long time, silent and uncomplaining as she'd always been.

She got the letter with the news of Francesca's death and came back to the town for the funeral, travelling a long distance from where she was now living. She thought, as she stood looking down at the body, that had she been allowed to become a nun, her sister would still be alive and in good health.

She went to see her brother-in-law after the burial. She strode in and, without waiting for him to disinfect the door-handle, began to call him all the names she could think of. He was, she said, a madman who was the laughing-stock of the whole town, an animal with disgusting personal habits in spite of all that stuff about microbes, just look at the beard encrusted with soup and snuff and snot, a sex-crazed swine, and of course, her poor sister had always been too meek and let him do what he liked with her, if she'd been in Francesca's place she'd have kicked him out of bed as hard as she could the moment he tried laying a finger on her, she would have whipped his bare backside with a willow branch, swish-swish-swish, and it would have been such a pleasure to hear him whimper like a puppy, begging her to stop. There was only one way of dealing with men like him – force their fly open, take it out, lay it flat on the table, get a chopping knife. Had he no mind of his own, the way he was forever running to priests for advice? Oh, it was easy enough for that lot to talk about sowing in the field, they didn't have to live with the consequences, and in any case there was no reason to look up to them, they were men like any others, worse in fact, everybody knew they had dirty minds, otherwise they wouldn't ask you the questions they did in the confession box.

He went white. 'You are the devil's daughter'.

She stood there, arms crossed, unperturbed. 'I'd rather', she said, 'be the devil's daughter than end up like my sister'.

He went to get his hunting rifle off the wall, and aimed it at her.

'I'm going to count up to ten', he announced. 'If you're not out the gate by the time I'm done, I'll start shooting'.

She walked towards the door, went down the steps and, having been silenced for the first and only time in her life, crossed the courtyard, opened the gate, closed it behind her, and was gone.

Cristina Cona was born in Turin, Italy, in 1951. She spent ten years in Ireland before moving to Brussels where she now lives and works as a translator.

Claire-Louise Bennett

Hand Me Down

It is not difficult to live amongst strange things and require nothing in the way of explanation. When I was a child one of my bath towels, a large white one, had the name Rebecca Teck stitched on to it, and I had a pair of what can only be described as bloomers with the name Ruth written on the elastic waistband in black felt-tip pen. As I answer to neither of these names and am without sisters you might be curious to know how it was I came to regard these items as my own. The easy answer would be to suppose I'd stolen them, but let's face it, what kind of person would I be if I stole other girls' bath towels and bloomers? Repeated use diminished any claim the names might have had, familiarity alone made them mine and I never wondered over those strange labels. I mention this as a note of caution. The nature of my curiosity is such that it does not look for reasons or causes or answers but prefers to uncover an area of certain mystery so that I can feel confident the world is truly unknowable. You, on the other hand are free to do what you please, and I anticipate you'll adhere to that peculiar and burgeoning trend of becoming an expert on someone else's life. You will see things where I cannot, because, as modern theory goes, I am too close to my own life to see it. But let me tell you this, my memory of visiting the Casino has no scent. It's a memory that visits me and I receive it as I would a guest, that is to say I am obliging, patient and courteous. Any inquisition is merely cursory, stemming from politeness rather than interest, and as such we are not so intimate that something might be disclosed. Looking for answers where there are none will undo you; obsession has no cure, not even the passing of time, and if you remember your dreams you will know that to be true.

You might imagine such a visit took place at night and involved a cab ride and fancy footwear, perfume, a velvet clutchbag and perhaps a male companion, but that's not how it was. Mother watered the plants, of which there were many, we ate a small lunch and left our house just after 3 o'clock. I wore a long silk and linen mix dress with a cropped jumper and tiny tiger-eye earrings. Clip-on earrings that did not hurt me so long as I kept them on. Of all the people I've walked with Mother was very possibly the best, as I tore about examining the world she continued at a steady pace in her own one. I was walking along a wall, which seemed to be accumulating more bricks as I went on, so that, before the end of it, I could see the plait coiled on my Mother's head better than I could see any feature on her face. And that is how she came to see my feet, which were bare. By now I was accustomed to her hand, not a day passed when I didn't feel it. I had learnt a great deal from the gentle application of her hand on my shoulder, my cheek, beneath my chin. I felt it now, the coolness of it, it caused me no alarm, there was no danger of me falling, I became still. 'You've nothing on your feet, do you think that'll be ok?' I put my arms back down by my sides and experienced the peculiarity of my position immediately, like a drop in the temperature. At the time my Mother was significantly taller than I and so I was used to tilting my head up to see into her eyes, but here I was standing with her nose level to my feet and so it seemed to me that I must reassure her in some way, indeed didn't her face search mine imploringly? 'Yes, I don't think anyone will notice. My dress is so long. If they see my toes, they will assume I'm wearing sandals'. She nodded and pulled at the hem of my dress, which was a little crinkled, and then she stepped away from the wall so that I could jump into her bare outstretched arms and return to size.

I was very glad to be back on the pavement and I think she was too, the sun had come out from behind a cloud and I wanted to gulp up some of its soft rays. In an effort to smooth out the goosebumps that I felt sure huddled on the back of my arms I ran in an idiotic manner to the traffic lights and pressed the button. I swung round the pole seven times before the man turned green. The man turned green just as Mother arrived at the kerb and she took my hand and although I noticed the man staring at her from his car she showed no acknowledgement, I slyly slipped my tongue out at him without her seeing. I don't remember feeling like I was on my way to a Casino, and the way I was carrying on, walking with one foot in the gutter and one hand on my head, would make it difficult for anyone to guess that that was where we were headed for. Although I moved faster than Mother I had the disadvantage of not knowing where the Casino was, which meant I had to turn and check her whereabouts more often than I would have liked. There was one occasion when I couldn't see her immediately, but then I spotted her profile and as I ran toward her it looked like she was kissing the wall of the Courthouse. In fact she had her hands cupped around a fossil in the stonework and she hoisted me up so I could do the same. The fossil tasted of fog. 'The world is very old', she explained and I wondered if she had been on it since the first day it was unwrapped and placed into the sky. A little while later we crouched down and prodded a dragonfly lying flat on its wings. 'It's as big as a bird' she said, and we fell back onto our bottoms in surprise when it quivered, a tremble that had nothing to do with any life left but owed everything to the breeze. 'It's been hit by a car' I said, and she looked over at the hot cars with so much sorrow I wondered if she might close down, but she spoke before I could think of anything she might like to hear, 'You wouldn't want it getting caught in your hair would you?' And I remembered the night down by the canal when it was very dark with only the smallest piece of moon leaning in the sky and I had made my hands into bats because she had sat so long without saying a word to me, without moving. Even so I hadn't meant for her to scream and I ran for a long time, not because I thought she would scold me, but because the sound that came from her frightened me and I wanted to hide from it. 'No you wouldn't' I agreed, but in honesty the few occasions when an insect has had the misfortune to entangle itself in my hair I have been remarkably calm. Sometimes you end up agreeing with something because you didn't hear the question properly, other times the manner by which you protest is so minuscule as to go unnoticed, and sometimes you acquiesce because you recognise how frail the world already appears to the person who is looking down into your eyes.

People frequently joke that while they are proficient at dispensing advice in the direction of others they are hopeless at getting their own lives in order. This is a fraudulent claim for two reasons, I've never found anyone's advice to be of any use to me, most times in fact they seem to identify a complaint I never knew I had, and secondly, people order their lives so scrupulously I imagine the inside pocket of their jacket contains footnotes typed meticulously on watermarked paper. I cannot deny that there have been moments in my life when much has altered very suddenly and on these occasions I have been quick to realise there can be no going back, and the only thing for me to do is to adapt and carry on.

I hadn't noticed my Mother pass me and felt a little pinch of panic when I whirled around a lamppost and saw she was no longer behind me. Always Mother is behind me. I looked at the traffic. I looked at the Courthouse and the place where the dragonfly lay drying up. It did not occur to me to look on ahead, I was surprised when I heard her voice behind me. She throws a whisper very well. 'Over here'. Like an arrow, like a hook, straight to me, opening in my ear like a flower overcoming shyness. By the way she stood on the bottom step I knew there was no more walking to be done. I knew that she would not want me to run towards her and I knew that when I got to her she would want me to press my fingertips onto her lips. She was wearing a red lipstick you see and on the few occasions she painted her mouth it was customary for me to blot her lips with my fingertips. I'd use both hands, and though I liked doing this very much my pleasure was always escorted by sadness. After I had blotted my Mother's lips it was usual for her to leave me. But she did not lower her face and she did not close her eyes, which was her usual signal that I should not follow, and my confusion increased when she extended her hand. Becoming unsure of everything I took it, but it could not stop the goosebumps from gathering on my arms again. Her head turned toward the entrance and she said, 'Keep your dress long', so I tugged at it with my free hand and followed her into the Casino.

You might imagine my eyes needed to adjust to the dark velvety interior, you might imagine large mirrors and chandeliers, gold fittings, glass tables and so on, but that was not how it was. Everything was white and smooth and clean and quiet, so so quiet. I remember feeling glad that I was not wearing fancy shoes because they would have made such a sound and as it was I felt self-conscious despite there being no-one around to see me, or indeed to hear me. Something about the walls told me that they had not heard the voice of a child so I kept quiet, which was just as well because I was certain that all the questions I wanted to ask would have done nothing but distract my mother. But I was very close to rebuking the authority of the white walls; my Mother's complete stillness made me frightened. Her eyes seemed to hang in her head and her hands had disappeared up her sleeves. I put my fingertips up to her mouth and she did not even bend down to make it easier for me. It must have been the sound of footsteps that startled her into closing her teeth around my fingertips. It did not hurt and I took them away only because I knew someone was approaching. A small woman walked towards us and all I remember of her was the colour of her eyes and how I could not imagine her voice ever leaving this white room, she smiled at me and said 'You have left footprints across the floor!' I looked behind me and thought, this is the opposite of snow and the way our prints collapsed into one another, fell open, got loose and disappeared. 'She's wearing sandals', my Mother says, as if it's the line of a song, the only one she can remember. But I don't want to go in to the Casino anymore so I shake my head and pull the crinkled hem up, and the small woman hovers an arm around my Mother's back as if she's waiting for my Mother to lean back and find the crease of her elbow-belly. And then my Mother snaps her eyes shut and I understand it's time for me to go and the lady with the eyes smiles again and my Mother's eyes are still closed. My Mother does not see me as I walk back across the floor in zig-zags. Of course I run home, of course I trample on the expired dragonfly, of course I punch the fossil, steady and unchanging in the Courthouse wall, and I do not know why.

There is nothing in that memory to confirm or even to suggest that where I left my Mother was a Casino and yet it is impossible for me to amend my memory. I don't expect you to support my decision, and the reason for that is obvious, I haven't told you anything but I'm certain that you've managed to interpret what little I have in a way that makes me want to rip out my tongue.

Claire-Louise Bennett was born in Wiltshire almost thirty years ago. She has lived in Galway for seven of those years and recently graduated from the university in Galway with an MA in Drama and Theatre. With a fellow graduate, she formed the theatre company Tooth and Nail. Their next project will be a devised piece exploring fear. This is the first story Claire-Louise has had published. She is currently working on a selection of short stories that examine the nature of victimisation.

Barty Begley

Hurling and Football

Rain clotted view. It is March. Like opposing outposts of an old war, he and his corner-back lean one against the other. He pitied him, equally as frightened and nervous as himself, having learned from some mean-spirited trainer, perhaps from his father, that the corner-back must keep his hurley against the man's back: he felt the constant nudging, the length of the stick against his shoulder-blades, or the butt occasionally into the middle of his back. This was done more for the form than out of any real conviction, and was just to be borne: he could move away all he wanted; his corner-back would always follow. He knew the type: pallid, blustering, afraid of everything, who suffered terribly during every game, having no desire to ever touch the ball, but enough sense of others' expectation to feel bound to make a show of trying to win it, and enough skill, whether innate or won through hours of lonesome slogging against the grey side-wall of the house, to occasionally get hold of it. He was shivering in the cold, holding by the one rule he remembered.

Was there still a war? A ball had been thrown into the mud some sixty yards away and had stayed there. The pelting rain kept from seeing any distance, and not one of the six full-backs and full-forwards in either team had come close to gaining possession. The going was too heavy for anything resembling hurling: solid rain. It is a trial match between under-14 selections from South Limerick and West Limerick, a trial for an eventual county Limerick team which will play in a weekend-long tournament at the beginning of the summer. Both he and his corner-back have lost interest and hope as half-time approaches, but neither speaks a word to the other, not even a word of complaint; it is too late now, and in any case both are too cold to speak.

His father drove him to the game and is now sitting in the car at the village end, the far end of the pitch. There is no way that his father can see him, and yet he is ashamed. His father has brought a friend along. Who is this friend? A light, grey man, with a flabby, heavily lined face, whom he has never seen before, and would never see again. At half-time, having never had a chance to even run for the ball, he is substituted. It is not surprising, as at least another ten hopefuls have waited on the sidelines in the rain, all through the first half. He makes his way to the car, without bitterness, wondering only whether his corner-back had also been substituted. He is from a very small club, and knows no-one else on the South Limerick selection. He changes in the car – he must have togged off there too – and the three sit looking out, other fogged-up cars around them, other fathers most likely, also pinned in by the weather. He sees that the car-park is separated from the field by a low mound, so that his father and his friend could not have seen the game from the car regardless of the weather. In good weather they would, he supposes, have stood out to watch. At club games his father always shouts loud encouragement and lambastment. He doubts whether he would have done so in the new and strange company. At this game no-one had shouted. There were no spectators, and the players were too nervous and cold to shout. It had been ghostly, and this lack of sound added to the isolation caused by the obscuring rain, and to the numbness caused by the cold, to furnish finally a sense of being alone in the world with his corner-back. Of course, at this moment they were in a cloud, hurling in a drifting cloud, but nobody sees and lives it that way. It is for them a sky as low as the grave, only worse because of hopes that it might lift.

His father does not really ask about the match; the friend murmurs sympathetically. In answer, he complains about his corner-back and corner-backs' tactics. Why does he do him that injustice? He had suffered alongside him, with him, and also because of him, but now that he had vanished, though perhaps still there in the rain, he could curse him. This was affirmation. They drove home, he silent, the two men silent for the most part.

Hurling is a game almost without structure. Each man ('or woman' is to be understood throughout) must simply beat his man as a part of a series of three or four such contests, and the final man have the wherewithal to do this and to put the ball between the posts. You can sometimes help the man next in this series by making a pass, but this is relatively rare. Almost every ball in hurling is a fifty-fifty ball, one man against his 'marker'; this a telling enough word. Each man is expected to win such contests. You are also expected to win forty-sixty balls. You win the ball, and then unless you are going for a score or making a pass, you play it as far as possible toward your opponents' goal. The succeeding contest in the series then takes place. Because of the thoughtlessness of such a process, hurling is a game of instinct and attitude, and, in the end, a game of desire. You are a link in a relatively homogenous chain of desire, your only struggle being with the desire of your marker. It is hard to be desirous in the cold and the mud, in any field of activity, and hard also when you become aware of your corner-back's personhood. Few things are worse in fact than marking a hurler only frightened into selfhood, whose sense of self does not encompass you and is reduced to his own expectation, oversensitive feelers searching for and touching the expectations of others, but ready to be pulled back at every moment. These are the hurlers who find no joy in anything, even in their own minor or major successes. These are the hurlers that injure you.

He was not called to further trials for the Limerick under-14 team, and in fact they had left well before the end of the game, when any arrangements as regards such trials might be announced. His father had said, peremptorily enough, 'Let's go', soon after he finished changing; the friend had raised no objection, and he was too disheartened to suggest waiting. He had wanted to. Is this how it must be: resignation? Vicious hope having to be suffocated?

At home the fire was lit; commiserations were proffered embarrassedly. He complained, rightly enough, of the impossibility of the conditions, and was supported in this by his father. This event, its loneliness, the deep green of the firs behind the goals washed to grey by the rain, the cement bench of the waiting substitutes, they a vague threat, unseen but felt, looking out from behind the sheets of rain, the unhappiness of his corner-back in his awareness of his self, all this soon faded and was subsumed by other successes and failures.

The rain had turned to a mist that hid the mountain as he went out in the early evening. He looked at it though he couldn't see it. He looked at the featureless grey and imagined that there were no mountains, but fields running to an infinite horizon, or a losing of lines of sight in ditches and trees. It was his job to clean out the cubicle house, a job he enjoyed, the methodicalness of the thing: animals out, stalls brushed down, centre aisle scrubbed out, lime sprinkled on the stalls, animals filtering back in tentatively, some, more canny than others, or simply more afraid of a cold day, pushing quietly in before he had finished. He was glad of them. Their smell was the calm, sweet smell of comfort, of refuge, the house warm with the body-heat of beasts at ease. In this house he had seen and assisted at manys a birth, a starry winter sky peering in through the tractor-high doorway. Were Joseph and Mary to seek shelter these days, it is here they would find it. As he sprinkled the stalls he eyed the dead crow hanging by its feet in the doorway.

Football is a different ballgame. Yes, fifty-fifty balls are an element, but much less so; it is about the team, about passing. The ball, quite simply, does not go as far, so your job in releasing it is to find a team-mate. Kicking as far as possible, though defended as a strategy by some die-hards, is only a last resort. You are thus forced to feel yourself part of a structured unit, to have a sense of your own responsibility as regards the outcome of the next one or two in the series of struggles for possession. Indeed, football is less a series of struggles than is hurling, and more a series of probabilities, almost inevitabilities, where only error will halt the successful progression of the series.

But he was corner-back. Corner-back in football is a purely negative force. He does not allow a corner forward to define himself, for a corner forward in football is not alone with his corner back as in hurling. The corner-forward in football is both utterly dependant on the one or two links before him in the series and creates these links, shapes and forms them, and even forges the link between them, by his own movement.

The corner-back in football is the loneliest player. He is absolute negativity: he is negative, but he is nobody's and nothing's negative. His identity is stopping a corner-forward, or at least it is if the corner-forward is good, but the corner-forward does not concern himself with the corner-back. Only a very bad corner forward will define himself by his relationship with his corner-back rather than by that with his team, but a good corner-back will know himself by his relationship with his good corner-forward, for whom he barely exists, and certainly doesn't matter. It is a hard position to play.

In football he was corner-back, and enjoyed it. Players in front of him depended on him for their sense of freedom; he knew they did, but he could not allow himself to take this into account, as this worth was born solely of the purity of his concern with his corner-forward. His absolute negativity, a negativity enclosed within itself, allowed his team-mates their freedom, team-mates and freedoms to which he must always be external.

In his first year on the senior team they played a grudge match against a well-touted side. The game of the previous year, from which the resentment had arisen, he had watched from the stands, a county final, in the Gaelic Grounds, watching in the first half, shouting in the third quarter and in the final quarter lamenting his half-parish's decline into unnecessary and self-defeating physicality. They had lost stupidly, and today was about proving their abilities, and yet more, about proving, and thus winning, self-possession.

They won, but there were no celebrations. In proving their worth, they – he felt included in this – had also demonstrated their culpability in the dissolution of the previous year. This day's curing of resentment, dipping and dropping of the sword of vengeance, need never have been necessary; they had shown that they could now only blame themselves. 'There is no fate', they said; 'there is agency, yours and others' or at worst there is lack of agency'.

They won that game but still lost, it being the last game in the opening, league-based, section of the county championship, and they already out of the running for qualification. They knew that the game had meaning only for their opponents, or at least only for their opponents meaning beyond itself as regards sport. For them it was not quite autotelic, but nearly, and they knew it. This winning and losing, or winning even though you have already lost, going out to win, honestly and sincerely desiring victory even though nothing is won – and when in fact innocence is lost, freedom from guilt, – is not uplifting, or cause for celebration for either player or spectator. If anything, the opposite: it is humbling to see a place and know it yours, not by fate, but by an act of your own. The talk later is of separate incidents, always a source of pleasure, but there is no future. There is only next year, and next year is not an easy thing in a small club with internal rivalries and reasons.

His father had been at that game, and had shouted with the rest, but unlike most he railed and congratulated in equal measure, regardless of affiliation. Watching Limerick play was the same. He tried to be chauvinist, tried to cheer only his own side, but he could not but acknowledge good play, participate in the joys of others as much as in Limerick's. Ground traced on a map and separated by a line – whether marking a river that only made for quarrels, or an arbitrary thing – it matters, he would be told, but a beautiful catch and clearance could override it. In football you have time to consider all this, or at least at corner-back, if your corner-forward is the static type, you sometimes catch yourself thinking about things. You shouldn't do; it ruins your game, and must be eliminated once spotted, but it does happen. To be a poet in a bunker is one thing, but if you think like a poet once out and about in battle, you had better hope that God loves poets, and history has not shown this to be the case.

That a friend of yours is from the parish you're playing, that the man being taken off injured has forty cows to milk, that to kill the thing you love is the worst of torments; any one of these thoughts can put you off your game. Thought is a tragedy: it is a flaw that both raises and destroys. A thinking footballer is no King Lear, but he rises by his vision, and then is laid low by it. A corner-back does not choose his corner-forward, but he must. He is the stoic who wants what happens. At the beginning of the game, he looks at his corner-forward and chooses him. The corner-forward has other concerns – such is his role, which he must also choose; his corner-back he does not need to choose. In hurling you do not need to make this choice; it is thrust upon you.

The spectators, on the other hand, are not made by the game, are in fact larger than it, as the Greek chorus is larger than the tragedy it comments upon. But a chorus can be implicated: the chorus turning about Eliot's Thomas-a-Becket, for example, is created by the tragedy; it is their tragedy. A gunslinger's wife also is the tragedy. She cannot flee what is woven in her. Hurling and football are shootouts: if you don't miss, you will usually win. But this is true for both parties. Does a gunslinger's wife actually cause her husband to be killed by her very fear? To train a hurling team is to be a gunslinger's wife. One cool evening in late summer he became the gunslinger's widow.

Playing into a setting sun, trains rolling by to the western end of the pitch, he could only stand and watch. In a game that nobody anywhere, nobody, remembers, a ball skidded across the square. Instead of pulling on it, someone went to lift it. That game is gone from memory; the bobbling ball is all that remains. And yet perhaps three hundred people saw that game. Where did it go? The result is in the sports pages of an archived newspaper somewhere. But of the game, all that is left is one moment. Why choose this moment? It was not necessarily decisive; that skittish ball perhaps made no difference. Something has to remain, of everything: a shard. It signifies nothing, as the thing, the game, is forgotten and means nothing. A signifier can only lead to another signifier. So if a thing is lost, it cannot be signified. What is this skidding ball, so? It is a shard, but a shard of what? The game is lost, forgotten; can it be a shard of that? No. A metonymy of error in general, of the chance of success, of the idea of the possibility of a wrong choice, of a right one.

A story told in some *History of Hurling* somewhere, or perhaps in the programme of an inter-county game, tells of an American seeing hurlers doubling on the ball above their heads, and declaring it to be the game of the gods. It is rather the very game of men, passing, fickle, delightful, heaping surprise on disappointment, awareness of oneself in others, on solipsism, surprise at oneself on surprise at oneself. This is the skidding ball, an onrushing consecutiveness of moments, perhaps decisive, perhaps not, of possibility, of possibility lost, a hurtling thing which can come and go, and where we both decide what we are and only struggle to know that which we are made to be.

Barty Begley lives in Galbally, South Limerick and in Montpellier, France

MAGS TREANOR

Framing the Past

I only said that I don't like your windows. And there you go again, defence and attack. I don't care if they're solid mahogany. I wouldn't know the difference between teak and Scandinavian pine. Plywood even, with a coat of varnish. All similar to this untrained eye.

I couldn't give a damn if the latches were gold plated, the hinges solid brass or the glass bullet-proofed. Alarm fitted even. Protection from this barking mongrel who doesn't have a neo-Georgian window frame to her name. Now listen this time. What I said is that I don't like your windows. I don't *like* them. Aesthetically speaking. Tired brown wooden squares turning the stretch in the evening into multiple triptychs.

But listening was never your medium.

Talking was mine and silence was yours. We compromised with touch. And in between touching I learned the sign language of your silence. Bottom teeth on your upper lip with insecurity getting the better of you. Get a life darling. Your responses grind like a wrong gear. You forgot to release the clutch, I can smell it.

'Did you have a good day?' 'yes'.

'Did you have a good day?' 'no'.

All I ever learnt about your days was that you had them. And your days became weeks spent recovering from weekends spent recovering from weeks.

When did I stop loving you and start liking the windows? When was it not fulfilling anymore to lie spread-eagled across your leather sofa, the afternoon sun a chessboard through the window? We kissed each other all through our lovemaking and I didn't care anymore about tomatoes/tomaytos, potatoes/potaytos. Your wicked dress sense was forgiven when you lay naked full of desire. This was a language we both shared, breasts all over the place and hungry cunts. A language where I became wild and passionate enough to forgive you for your John Denver CDs.

Was it the book club stopped me loving you?

Those politically correct, uppity, respectable women. The clitorati in their Birkenstock sandals. Pigging out on academic apple pie and fresh herbs from your garden, plumply plámásing one another on their intellectual prowess. No, it wasn't the book club. And it wasn't your two gay men friends who came to dinner, bringing cake in a Tupperware box. I believe I offended them. How could I not? Their nice respectable lady friend was a paint by numbers relationship and I was the graffiti. Not that I felt that way about it myself. It was you who were controversial. Sweeping mountains under carpets for small talk at tea. But the cake was delicious.

And it couldn't have been your cooking, your singing, your forgetting things. You forgot to smile; you forgot your glasses, your phone, yourself most of the time. But you struggled hard and worked well on things that didn't come naturally. I admired you for that.

Your bedroom was home to plaid flannel sheets, hot water bottles and glaring reading lamps, while mine donned pure silk, a broken chair for a bedside locker and heaps of candles giving birth to dark brown circles wherever the metal shell of a tea-light made love to a virgin windowsill. Landmarks recorded only in the histories of rented accommodation.

But we were always naked, and ready and fighting. I loved you even more on my territory. The low bed with no headboard, creaking and moving away from the wall. The so-called en-suite: a windowless cupboard housing a shower and toilet. Never a clean towel and always out of toilet paper. And the luxury of wrestling with you, as you tried to conquer my side of the bed. 'You're power hungry, I think you've got issues' I said, 'but I like your knickers'.

For some reason, I wanted you, and we compromised with touch. We compromised with silence, and words, with words that created silence and silence that stretched into words. Words like 'I love you' choked the silence of 'lust'. 'I love you, I love you' – I love your knickers when I'm pushing them down your leg with my foot. I love your big breasts sailing across my face, my lips. I love your hands when they go places I can't see anymore. I love you.

But I hated your windows. You had a window for me. That's what you used to say, calling me at times convenient only to you. 'I have a window, we could do coffee'. And I would jump. Pushing a child from my breast or removing a dentist from my tooth. She has a window. A window. We ate cake when there was no bread, and I was starving. Thank you for your window but it's a whole house I need.

Because you see, Darling, I said that I don't like your windows. It's me, not you. You loved the backdrop of a thousand triptychs, a curtain to wrap yourself in. Something to muff the sound of shattering glass as I put my foot through it. No mosaic to piece together this time. I'm not insured and I refuse to pay. Yes, that was when I stopped loving you. Looking back and hearing a noise that was greater than the damage. Something you had never told me about your windows. That they could only get broken in little sections.

Mags Treanor was born in 1965. Originally from Dublin, she now lives in Galway where she writes fiction, short stories and prose, and is also currently working on a novel. Her work has been broadcast on the Marian Finucane Show on RTÉ Radio One and is soon to be published in the *Harrington Lesbian Fiction Quarterly*, a Haworth publication.

JOHN O'REGAN

Moonshine

I guess we grew up like savages on account of us living in the countryside. My brother Mick and me were the youngest and no one cared too much what we got up to. There were nine of us and we figured we had four big sisters to do the housework so we could do whatever we wanted. We didn't care and anyway our mother was dead and sometimes we drove our eldest sister crazy and she beat us cos it didn't matter to us if we went to school with no shoes on. Even then me and my brother knew there were important things in life and whether you wore your shoes to school or not wasn't one of them.

Our father was hardly ever there. We'd see him in the evenings after he'd come in from working on the roads or from one of the other things he did like thatching or repairing people's boots or snaring rabbits. He snared a lot of rabbits and then he'd tie them to a stick and carry them around the farms to sell them or trade them for something to feed us with. He caught salmon too or poached them, I don't know what you call it, except that it would have been a bad thing if he was found doing it. Anyway, he caught a lot of them too and there was no shortage of either rabbits or salmon, along with potatoes that he'd dig up from the field behind the house. My father was always up to something that had to do with feeding us or keeping a roof over our heads and didn't have much time for Mick and me and the things we got up to.

Once, when I was fourteen, he said I was going to be going to America . He said his brother had written from Texas offering to take one of us off his hands and that I'd be the one to go since I had such a bad temper that people would be scared of me and leave me alone, and that way I wouldn't get molested or whatever it is happens to you when you're on your own like that on a big ship or on a train. I didn't know what any of it meant and didn't care too much either except the part where I'd have to leave Mick all alone in that house with those crazy sisters of ours. But I forgot about that too when my father brought me into town to get me some new clothes and a new coat. Like I said, I was fourteen by then and was starting to care about clothes and things. I got new shoes too. They were black and had a strap across the front and were as shiny as hell but I wasn't allowed to wear them until the day I was going and had too leave them in the box they came in under my bed.

It wasn't easy saying goodbye to Mick. He got all sulky and I knew he was sad. While I was going down the road for the last time I was hoping he'd show up to wave goodbye but when he didn't I knew he'd be up on the hill sitting on some clump of grass, stabbing his penknife into the ground or knocking stones together to hear the echo off the cliff on the far side of the river. It was a while before I'd be able to leave him, sitting there, alone, in my mind I mean. I was always going back there that way, just sitting beside him waiting for the echo to come back or maybe pegging stones at rabbits. He had his own life after that, after he went away. It was a long, hard life but at least he had one and he thought about me sometimes too because we wrote each other for a while after until he stopped and went on to someplace else and my letters couldn't find him any more.

My father's last words to me before I got on the boat were to remind me not to speak to anyone till I got to Texas. This time I was the one who couldn't wave goodbye because I was in my cabin and I was crying. I don't want to talk too much about the trip since I was sick most of the time. I was lonely too because I couldn't talk to anyone. Some people tried to talk to me but I avoided them, even though they looked just like me and were probably harmless enough. Mostly I just hung around at the railings with my hands in my pockets, clutching onto my passport with one hand and the other holding onto the twenty five dollars that I needed to get into America at the time, and every hour or so, I'd feel for the ticket inside my coat, just to be sure it was still there. My sisters had bought me some comics and I spent my time reading them over and over again until I nearly had them worn out.

Anyway I don't want to talk too much about that either, or about the Statue of Liberty or Ellis Island or what I saw of New York. My father had told one of the stewards to look out for me so he put me straight onto a bus that took me to the train station where I got a night sleeper to Chicago, then I had to find my own way to another train to take me to Houston. It was on that train that something happened to make me sad, well sad at first then kind of relieved. I was in my bunk in one of the sleeper carriages on account of it taking nearly four days to get to Houston. Anyway, I had taken off all my clothes, folded them neatly, put them in the case at the end of the bunk and put on my nightshirt. Then I closed the lid and put my shoes on top. Let me say that I'd never seen a black man before, a few in the train station but never before that I mean and certainly never up close.

Anyway at about 4 o'clock in the morning this black man parted the curtains, reached into my bunk and took my shoes, I mean he just reached in, felt around a bit in the dark, found my new shoes and took them. Well I must have been saving it up because I don't think a human being has ever cried as much as I did when that happened. The sheets were soaked, the pillow was soaked, my nightshirt was soaked, and that wasn't the end of it either because then you know what happened? He brought them back again, polished. Well that started me up all over again. I swear I held onto those shoes for dear life after that and they must have looked a sight by the time I got to Houston because he never got to polish them again, ever, I'm telling you he didn't.

I kind of recognized my Uncle Dan on the platform in Houston. I'd met him, once, at about the time he was leaving for America and he looked more or less the same, but big, real big, bigger than any man I'd ever seen. It was like there was so much space around him that he'd had to grow taller and wider in order to fill some of it up. He just lifted my heavy suitcase like it was nothing and I tagged along behind him till we got to his car. It was a nearly brand new Model T Ford. He'd worked himself up to being a foreman on the Santa Fe Railroad and I figured he must be about the richest person I'd ever met. I climbed in the back with my Aunt Winnie who was from around where I was born and she says I just started up talking and didn't quit for a week.

When we got to their house it was the prettiest house I'd ever seen. It had a porch with a swing and flowers around it and a dog who jumped up on me and there was some kids next door who looked about my age who turned out be Polish and there was a big pitcher of iced tea on a table inside with a clean white table cloth and my own room and everything was clean and so much new stuff all around that I could hardly take it all in. My Aunt had no children of her own and just kept hugging me all the time until I was bruised all over. Then she'd sit there, grinning, drinking her iced tea and letting me get on with telling her about all the things that had happened on my journey or about the family back home or even about the first thing that came into my head.

It took a while to get used to the iced tea I'll tell you. And other things too, like the big bowls of chilli and biscuits that my uncle ate all the time, on account of the hot weather he'd say. Then there was the heat that made everything sort of damp with fungus growing everywhere and my Aunt at her wit's end trying to keep it out. There was no breeze coming off a river either or anything that might help to keep you cool. The nearest thing to a cool breeze we'd get is if we went out to the levee with a picnic on Sundays where they'd watch me swim with some of the other kids while one of the men would sit off to one side with a shotgun in case there were any alligators lurking around.

Of course I was keeping an eye on the boys as well but most of the ones that were the right age for me, like a few years older, had joined up and were only around once a month, since their training was really tough and anyway they were about to be shipped over seas, to the Western Front my Uncle said. Later I was expected to wave them off with a little flag from the platform along with the rest of the school, not that I was in school for too much longer. After I left school I got a job with Hughes Tool, making engine parts for airplanes. Later I found out the owner, Mr. Hughes himself, was one of the richest men in the world and he lived on the top floor of some hotel and grew his fingernails so long he couldn't hold his fork and his toenails and beard too and eventually stopped eating anything except ice cream and just faded away to nothing. There isn't much I can say about that except it's probably not all that strange and could even happen where I come from, and maybe did, once or twice.

You'd have to be dumb not to be able to get by in Houston in those days. There was plenty of work for someone who wanted it so I moved around and was a telephone operator once and then worked as a secretary in a company called Foley Brothers and all the time I was growing up and getting my own things and my own life and going to church and learning how to get by. Another thing I had to get used to was the Black folks. I always got on well with them and sometimes used to sneak into their church to hear them singing cos they were the best singers in the world but if I got too friendly something would be said or someone would look over their shoulder at me at church and I'd start to feel uncomfortable or some little thing would happen and the message would be clear. If the Klan were on the prowl everyone knew to stay indoors but my uncle was a big man and he wasn't scared of them and they knew it. He was well respected round abouts but the Klan weren't just after the Black folks and at one time they started lynching Catholics as well, so the local priest would often come to our house in the middle of the night and I'd have to get up to let him in. I got so used to it that I never thought too much about it. There'd be a gentle knock on my window and I'd get up and let him in and give him a glass of whiskey and arrange the sofa in the living room so's he could get down behind it with a few blankets. Then he'd watch the lights of the cars going across the walls as the Klan searched up and down the street for him, never getting any sleep of course and being a total wreck in the mornings. One night, he got word they were looking for him and after I'd done the usual thing with the whiskey and the sofa there was a knock at the door. I woke my Uncle and he opened the door to find this young kid standing on the porch saying there'd been an accident on the highway and could the priest come and my Uncle said, Don't go, it's a trap, but the priest said No, he had to, it was his duty, and he left with the young kid and nobody ever saw him ever again.

About that time the men were getting down in the dumps cos they were told they couldn't drink no more alcohol until it got so bad they started up making their own out of corn mash. They called it Moonshine and once a neighbor told my Aunt that if she didn't want her dog to grow no bigger she should pour some Moonshine down its throat and she did and the dog disappeared under the house and we didn't see it again for the longest time and figured we'd poisoned it or the snakes had got it.

Not long after that I was walking down the street and this nun that I knew came running up to me, all out of breath, and asked if I seen the good looking Irishman who was around and sometimes came to the church to pray. I said I hadn't but would look out for him and started hanging around the church to see if I could catch a glimpse of him. About a week or so later this fella walked past me as I was coming out of the store and I figured that must be him so I followed him and sure enough, he went to the church and knelt down with his head in his hands. I thought he looked a bit shabby with the soles of his boots worn through but he was saying his prayers so at least that was a good sign.

Anyway, his name was Frank and we got married about a year later and then the Big Depression came and things went from bad to worse until there was just about no work for anyone and a lot of people had to rely on soup kitchens if they didn't want to starve. Frank got wind there was work to be had picking fruit in California so he headed off, hoboing on the box cars, till he got to the Napa Valley where he picked oranges and peaches during the fall. He'd turn up a few weeks later, always at night and he'd be infested with fleas and lice after travelling on the box cars all the way, so I'd have to get a bath ready for him in the back garden filled with stuff that killed off everything and then I'd pick up his clothes with two sticks and put them on a termite mound out on the prairie behind the house and the termites would have them cleaned out by the morning. After that we had a little girl called Sadie and I got a camera around the same time so there's lots of photographs of Sadie growing up and all her school friends coming round in their pretty dresses. There's one that shows them carrying a big basket of ornaments that they'd collected in the houses up and down the street cos they were things that were marked 'Made in Japan' and they'd just heard about Pearl Harbor on the wireless. They figured they were doing something for the war effort by going out onto the street and smashing up all the ornaments and I had to go out that night and sweep it all up again in case the cars were damaged or the glass cut up the horses hooves cos there were still cowboys in those days who would come into town to get drunk and then the horses would know to stand next to a lamp post so the cowboys could lean against it and fall asleep.

It wasn't long before we decided we'd like to come home again and we came home on the Queen Mary and could hear the orchestra playing two decks above us in the night and it was lovely to watch the sun go down and listen to Beethoven or whoever it was and the rich folks all laughing and dancing and drinking champagne probably. We'd put a bit of money together by then and we bought a small sweet-shop in Dublin but neither of us knew too much about running a shop so it went bust within a year and soon after that we were in a town square somewhere in the midlands, surrounded by our cases, tossing a coin in the air to decide if we'd go north or south. I'll always remember it came down on heads because that meant we'd be going south and I have to say I'm glad cos that was nearer to where I come from and at least I'd be able to visit relatives and maybe Sadie might meet someone and I might know the family cos she was 17 by then and had big long legs and was pretty as a picture.

Anyway, a lot more stuff happened after that like Frank dying cos he never had any luck and started drinking or else he'd have a little bit of luck and not enough for everything to fit together so's it would lead somewhere. I'm 84 now and I live with Sadie and her family and mostly I watch my grandchildren grow up and tell them things they don't know about and hopefully will never need to know about either. Sometimes I think my mind has turned to stone from all the things I've seen and done and I wouldn't be able to fit too much more in except I like to watch the crows flying past the windows and can nearly tell everything that's going on in the world from the way they're standing on a branch or trying to stay up in the sky if the wind is blowing hard or there's a hurricane or whatever it's called. They gave me a pension and I've been putting some of it away every week over the last few years to buy a plot in the graveyard and I suppose I'll be lying down there pretty soon and that will be all there is to it. So now I've just been reading back over this and wondering if there's a lesson to be learned from it all that I could tell you about but I can't see anything except life is for living and when all is said and done you might as well get on with it. Things happen to you and they keep happening and then you get to the age I am and they slow down a bit and then stop and there's nothing left except the crows and some old photographs and maybe showing the kids how to make iced tea and them hating it the way I did when I tasted it first. I guess I can't think of anything else for now and really I don't suppose it matters all that much anyway cos mostly you just have to figure it out all by yourself.

John O'Regan is originally from Waterford and now lives in Galway . His work has been included in many journals, most recently in the re-launched *Stinging Fly*. He is also a visual artist and is at present working on a Barna Woods series.

DRAGO JANCAR

Jump off the Liburnia

Translated from Slovenian by Lili Potpara

'Jump'.

He was standing about a metre from the edge. The dark surface below was moving rapidly. He was standing about a metre from the edge of the ship's side, with one hand holding the rail at his back, looking at the water surface quickly moving past. His other hand swayed, and with it his slightly bent body.

'Jump', she said.

It was night, the shell of the sky closed by clouds above, the dark surface below. Perhaps it vibrated slightly; perhaps it moved along the sides of the ship like the back of a big animal. In the air there was the smell of smoke, which trailed from the wide muzzle of the funnel above them. There was no wind, but the smoke was nevertheless being pushed downwards, so that from time to time he felt its sharp smell in his nostrils, mixed with the fragrance of water, possibly of salt.

'Jump', she said, and her quiet, careless voice cut through the middle of his body and settled on top of his stomach. He could feel that something was actually drawing him down, into the depths. The feeling had emerged a moment before, maybe a minute before, a minute before he jumped over the rail and took a step away from her, towards the dark, rapidly moving abyss. A minute before he had been stretched on a deck chair, his feet by the edge of the rail; a minute before he had been smoking a cigarette. A minute before he had tossed the burning cigarette end over the rail, he had watched the flashing dot hang in the darkness for a moment, sway, and then draw a bright arc downwards. It seemed to him that he could hear a hiss on the surface. Of course, nothing hissed, nothing could be heard apart from the smooth hum of the ship's engine. It only disappeared; something, which a moment before had been in his hands, disappeared completely and finally, and after it disappeared, there was nothing left, neither in the air, nor in the water, nor in the darkness in which the ship was sunk. Into which they were both sunk, stretched in canvas deck chairs at the side of the ship, after dinner, without speaking, with vacant eyes staring into the darkness towards where the shore was supposed to be, where the shore actually was, since twinkling lights emerged there and disappeared again, on the shore, perhaps deep inland.

'Say it again', he said.

He tore his gaze from the lights on the shore and felt rather than saw the dark surface of the sea, the deep plane; his heart started beating faster. The feeling which lay on top of his stomach rose towards his heart, towards the hollow inside, towards the hammering in the middle of the body's hollow space, and the dangerous, frightened thought whizzed through his brain that he might actually jump; if she said it just once more, he would have no strength left to step back. She must feel it; this is not a game any more. If only a moment before, when he had followed the cigarette end with his eyes, when he had stood up and climbed over the metal rail, if it had all been a prank, then now, suddenly, everything was at stake. She must feel he is being drawn into the abyss; she must get up and hug him; she must at least be quiet. She was quiet. But it was not enough any more. Let her feel the fear running through him, for God's sake; let her be humiliated only for a moment; let her beg him, ask him to move. Why is she lying behind his back motionless, wrapped in a blanket? Why does she not, with a single gesture, put a stop to all the misunderstandings which have accumulated during the last few years in their lives? Let her utter just one word and the sudden madness will be cured, they will both be cured. He could feel that in this long moment she was probably thinking, judging his readiness for risk. It seemed to him that she had moved. She must get up, she must say a word, this will be a word of concern for him, a word of love and salvation. Let her at least say, you are behaving like a child; let her say, stop this nonsense; let her say, it's cold, let's go down into the cabin; let her say, the water is cold; let her make a joke, let her laugh, let her cough, let her yawn. He let go of the rail and his hands hung by his body, he bent his head. Where is the froth? Is it behind the ship? Where are the waves? Have they been swallowed up by the dark? He could feel her breathing behind his back, her eyes fixed on his nape. They were alone; a few young people were asleep in their sleeping bags, sheltered from the wind at the bow of the ship; no body could be seen, no hand or head stretched, withered corpses wrapped in silky textile. Say a single word, he thought, and you will be forgiven everything, I will be forgiven everything, everything we have done to each other in recent years; I'm sorry for everything, I'm really sorry, just say a word, he thought. This is not humiliation, or, is it humiliation if you take a step towards me, a single step? After so many years of marriage, after so many wounds, just a word; say, this is a silly provocation; say, one shouldn't play with things like this, shouldn't stand at the edge of the ship, shouldn't look down. Down into the intoxicating, crazily intoxicating depth which wants to draw one to it, flatten one on it, pull, sink to the dark bottom.

'Jump', she said.

My God, he thought, my God, now I'll really jump.

Actually, I'll just take a step forward, a step too many. Now I really feel dizzy, he thought. Now he can no longer think, what a horrible provocation, what has actually happened, why is he standing here being drawn over the edge? He cannot think of anything; everything has gone quiet – the ship and the engine, the beating of his heart in his chest and head – only the echo of the silence remains. He stepped to the very edge and swayed dangerously. I'm a good swimmer, he thought, nevertheless, at fifty I'm still a good swimmer; will the siren blow, will I be pulled under the ship? It seemed to him that she had got up. He desperately turned round; she had not got up. With the corner of his eye he caught the dishevelled head of a stranger, she poked it from the sleeping bag, the startled eyes of a girl. A mouse out of flour, he thought, and clung to the thought, a mouse out of flour; why do we say a mouse out of flour? How does a mouse look out of flour, what has a mouse looking out of flour to do with that dishevelled head, with the sleepy astonished unknown girl's eyes looking out of a sleeping bag? There's nothing I can say. I'll jump now, I'll step over the edge and a moment later it'll be all over. I can't do anything, I mustn't say anything, everything is hollow and quiet and crazily frightened, and yet decided. Say nothing.

'I'm saying it for the last time', he said, 'say it for the last time'.

Because of the gaze, transfixed by the dark running surface, the depth, because of the magnetism drawing him down, because of the something with no name, his body started trembling. What is it, he thought, am I drunk? They had drunk a bottle of wine over dinner. Will I swim out? I'm not drunk, I won't swim out. The thought was looking for an exit in fast, energetic thrusts. The sea is the Adriatic, the ship is the *Liburnia*, we are wife and husband, many years at the edge, now I'm standing at the edge, in the distance, on the shore, there is light, the depths are dark, the ship is wrapped in darkness. Sometimes, when he stood on the tower by the pool, on a rock by the sea, when the tiny boy's shuddering body, the frightened trembling soul, wanted to show his friends that he dared, that he really dared, he used to count, count to three, and then he always jumped: when he started counting he knew he would jump, although he knew there would be terrible moments of absence during the fall, that it might hurt down below, the impact on the surface.

Now it was different, everything was the same, but nevertheless different. The point now was to spring into the heart, not into the sea, his heart and hers, the heart in which everything began and acquired its sense. But to accomplish this, she must utter a word, a single word; it must not be a humiliating word, it must not be the ironic: jump, it must not be: jump-because-of-me, it must not be his failure at this edge, this moment, can she not feel it in her chair, wrapped in a blanket, this moment life can start anew. This moment his body is trembling, can she not see it, this moment he is really irresistibly being drawn to the depths. The brief laughter of young people drifted from the deck, a door slammed, a discarded bottle rushed past in the sea, the dome of the cloudy sky lowered. He felt his palms were sweaty; beads of cold sweat emerged on his forehead, cold wind started blowing and again he could feel the stinking smoke from the ship in his nostrils. Will this be the end, the last sensory perceptions he will take over the edge, into the emptiness, into the dark? Or will she now say a word, another word?

'I'm saying it for the last time', he said, 'say it for the last time'. He said it twice, it was like counting to three in his boyhood years, he said it twice, at short intervals he answered quickly, angrily, challengingly, humiliatingly, now is three, a moment later I say three, I'm saying it for the last time, he said, say it for the last time.

'Jump', she said quietly.

She said it quietly, she said it with a quieter voice, and this stopped him for a moment. But at the same instant the thought caught up with the brain that she had said it, said it despite everything, she had said what she should not have said for anything in the world, and he sprang over the edge. Actually, he did not spring, he had no strength left for that. He simply took a step forward; he simply moved his foot and collapsed into the dark empty space. To tell the truth, he did not step into the deep void, he slipped into it. He sat at the edge, clutched the metal frame with his hands and slid along the edge towards the rapidly approaching, larger and larger, more and more painful surface of the sea. No ground under the feet, nothing to hold on to, he flew through space, through the dissolved and supple airy matter. The cloudy dome of the sky and the blue-black surface of the sea were turned upside-down and merged. Now the sky was below, then it was carried away and blurred; now something gradually rose in his chest, then his heart was captured by its own trembling which at the same time was the trembling of the air through which he flew. Everything was visible and yet invisible, the direction of the fall was simultaneously up and down, the curve of the horizon was rounded, gravity was derailed, the unity of the world became denser and at the same time open, the water and the air, the sea and the sky.

The bodily matter disintegrated on contact with the immobile surface of the sea. For a moment he could see the light on the shore towards which he was supposed to swim; for an instant he saw the immense shadow of the ship, its metal side, its dark body rushing past, dragging him towards it. He heard a scream, a shrill when he heard the roaring of the ship engines, their coughing and stopping, the grumbling signal siren; when he heard it all he was far behind, in the middle of the spuming waves the monster was leaving behind, far below without vision or hearing, without breathing or pain, enclosed in the watery matter, the disappearance, the prenumbness.

She was still lying wrapped in a blanket, now, by the white metal wall, in the dark. She lifted her head only slightly. The girl with the dishevelled hair and mousey, tiny, sleepy eyes lit a cigarette. She raised her head only slightly to see him more clearly clutching the metal rail, murmuring something into his chin. He did not swing himself over the edge, he did not move his foot and with a single step fall into the void, he did not slide along the side of the ship towards the rapidly approaching, larger and larger, more and more painful surface of the sea.

He did not jump. He did not spring into the centre, the heart, the place where everything began and acquired its sense. He did not throw himself anywhere. He stood by the rail and felt that his trembling body was calming down, that the hollow void in his head and chest was filling with noises, senses, looks. The ship alone was shuddering with the jolts of the engine, the sharp, stinking smoke was filling his nostrils; he looked towards the shore and watched the approaching lights of a town. I'll hit you, he thought, I'll kill you. Down in the cabin, if not here, then down in the cabin.

'How could you', he said, 'how could you?'

A warm wind started blowing from the shore. The lights of the town were approaching. If he had turned he would have seen that, despite the warm wind from the shore, she had pulled the blanket up to her chin. If he had turned he would have seen there was nevertheless a hint of surprise and uncertainty in her eyes. Not fear, simply uncertainty and surprise. This would have sufficed. But he did not turn.

'What does *Liburnia* actually mean?' she said quietly.

He was silent. How could you, how could you?

'You don't know?' he said. 'It was an ancient Illyrian kingdom.

You don't know?'

'It's cold', she said after a while, 'let's go down'.

It was not cold, it was warm; warm wind blew from above the stony hills, with piles of stones on top, ancient Illyrian graves. There it probably roared and howled around the peaks, from there it blew clouds above the water, here it dissolved into a soft mass of air above the sea surface which was suddenly no longer an oily, quiet surface but a slightly wrinkled one, with frothy crests in places. The girl in the sleeping bag drew a few more puffs from the cigarette, then she threw the burning end over the rail, into the dark. The wind held it for a while, then forcibly carried it along the side of the ship, back and down. The

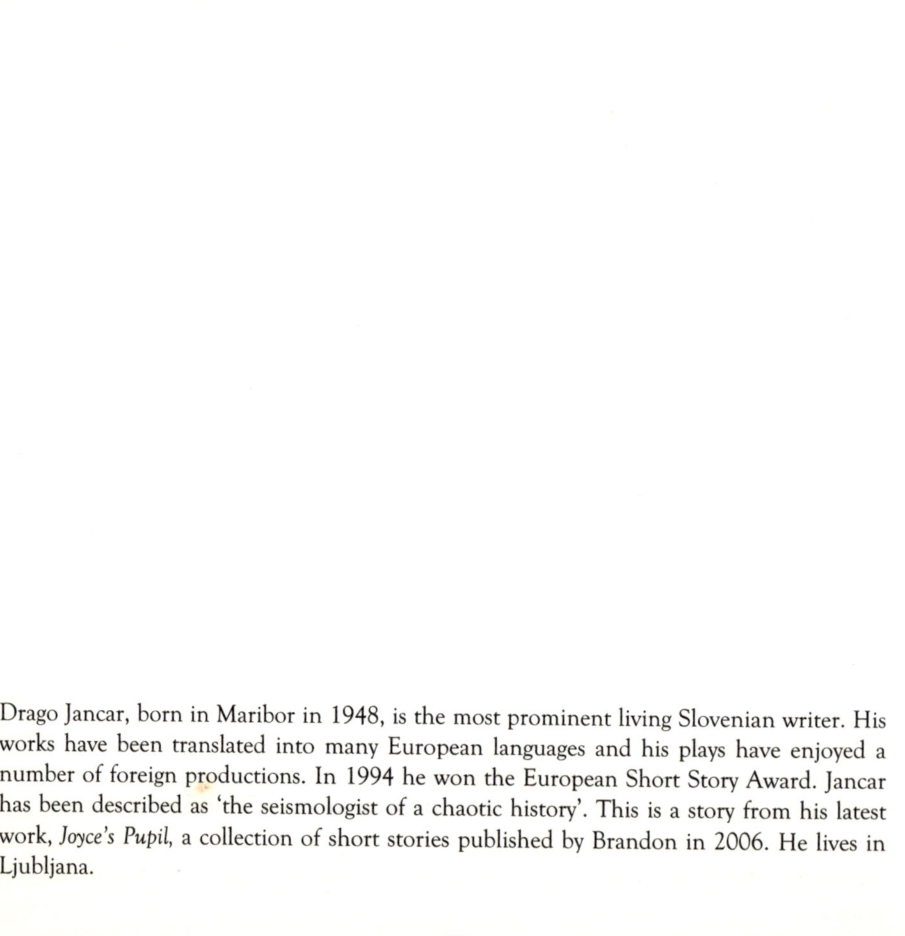

dishevelled hair disappeared. She zipped up the sleeping bag over her head.

'Let's go down', he said. 'Let's go now'.

Drago Jancar, born in Maribor in 1948, is the most prominent living Slovenian writer. His works have been translated into many European languages and his plays have enjoyed a number of foreign productions. In 1994 he won the European Short Story Award. Jancar has been described as 'the seismologist of a chaotic history'. This is a story from his latest work, *Joyce's Pupil*, a collection of short stories published by Brandon in 2006. He lives in Ljubljana.

LIONEL SHRIVER

An Excerpt from *Double Fault*

'I don't think so ... No, Tuesday's my first wedding anniversary, but that's not the problem. I just think we've reached the end of the road, John. If the game's no longer competitive, there's no point. I've got some other names if you – ... Yes, they are my 'discards', if you insist on – ... Hello?' Eric put down the phone. 'Bastard hung up on me'.

Their Manhattan apartment, being affordable, was small; his wife Willy couldn't help but listen in. 'Can you blame him? I thought John Lance was a friend of yours'.

'He wasn't a friend, he was a hitting partner. You should know the difference'.

Well, she did. Eric's childhood list of what he wanted to be when he grew up was long as his arm – and a long, tendinous arm that now was. Willy never had a list. All she'd ever wanted to be from the age of five was a professional tennis player. Accordingly, by twenty-four she'd been scything her way through tennis chaff most of her life, and was if anything better acquainted with the disposability of hitting partners than Eric, who had only decided (a little capriciously, in Willy's private view) to mount the tennis ladder at twenty-two.

The decorative preliminary natter about romances or weather camouflaged the utilitarian character of the sports 'friendship'. Beyond a post-match beer, itself only tolerable if the score was close, hitting partners were rarely invited into your social circle. Because hitting partners got used up. But Willy had never seen anyone consume as many partners in such short order as her own husband. Eric chewed them up and spit them out, ingesting morsels of strategy or technique along the way as he sucked oysters from a chicken back and left the bones.

'Why not beg off that you're out of town?' Willy suggested. 'Anything but, *Your game stinks, don't call again*'.

'He'd know I was making excuses. I double-bageled him our last match. John's ranking will never rise from the late 700s'.

'You were in the 700s six months ago. Why now the pee-yew?'

'Because I'm pushing to the 400s by early next year', Eric explained impatiently. '*You* can't bear partners you shellac'.

'There's just something hideous about telling someone point-blank that they're not good enough for you anymore'.

'This is a ruthless sport'.

'Which brings out a side of you that makes me nervous'.

'What should make you nervous is if out of some misplaced altruism I keep playing inferiors and bring my progress to a standstill'.

'What if John improved?' she pressed. 'Games wax and wane. He might overtake you again'.

Eric snorted. 'Never happens'.

It never happened. Eric had yet to be surpassed by any opponent over whom he'd established dominion. In no endeavor had Willy's husband ever experienced a stall, much less a setback. The prospect of regression was as preposterous to him as the notion of waking up two inches shorter. Willy had been in the pro game two years longer, and she herself knew the brief, shuddering horror of watching your ranking slip the wrong direction for a month or so. She had shared a locker room bench with plenty of has-beens, once in the top-200 and wandering, bewildered, in the wasteland of the 800s. They all had a distinctively stunned, battered look, like accident victims in shock. Particularly to Americans, for whom life was definitionally a series of betterments, a shift into reverse defied some hitherto immutable rule of physics – as if time itself had run backwards. Regression was betrayal, bequeathing the shaken trust of earthquake survivors, for whom the solidity of the very earth is newly unreliable. But the ground under Eric's feet had never rumbled; his second-hands plowed unremittingly clock-wise. While his innocence gave him power, it accorded him a callousness as well.

'So I boot some no-talent from my list', said Eric. 'Why does that rattle *you*?'

'Maybe you plan on going through wives the same way', she said dryly. He laughed, but she hadn't meant to be funny.

Eric raised his slender wife by the armpits, extending his arms until her pale, fly-away hair grazed the ceiling. 'I *use* hitting partners. I *love* you'.

She supposed that made her lucky; Willy was officially the object of Eric's whole ardour. He wasn't very interested in friendship. Since their marriage, he had failed to keep up with his old roommate, and never evinced any enthusiasm about dinner parties or having someone over for a drink. If she did arrange a social occasion, he got annoyed. They were both on the road, different roads, for such a fat chunk of every month that Eric was possessive of intersections with Willy and stingy with their evenings. He was an absolutist, and valued efficiency. Eric had invested all his passion in his wife, like sinking his life-savings into a single stock.

The lack of diversity in Eric's emotional portfolio, while not an imposition precisely, was a responsibility. Eric had no other Great Love. Tennis for Willy's husband had clinical, strictly geometrical aspect. Though in matches he often deployed stoicism as a weapon, Willy wondered if on the most profound level he really didn't feel much on the court. Eric liked winning, of course, but regarded tennis as the mere instrument by which victory was achieved; it had little value itself except as a framework for raw contest. The game never sent him careening on the tempestuous roller coaster of rapture and desolation that for Willy served as a parallel romance. So entranced by her profession, Willy sometimes felt irrationally unfaithful, just as Eric could become irrationally jealous of her enthrallment with a sport to which he was presumably devoted himself.

Like so many men, Eric respected only those who thrashed him. Once he'd wrested the advantage, his interest dwindled. He grew derisive and restive when vanquished adversaries called, irritable when their appointments came due, until finally with a crumple he tossed their numbers in the can. Ever ravenous, Eric was fond of stalking tennis courts for choice, unravaged talent. Every month or two he would return from these safaris clutching a new phone number, wearing the grin of a tom chomping a live mouse, with which he planned to toy before the kill.

It was on just such a predatory prowl of Riverside Park's northern courts that Eric had pounced on his wife-to-be. Willy had first caught his eye by dispatching a passably competent amateur in two slam-bam, take-no-prisoners sets. (She'd have drawn out the match longer just for the delight of thumping the ball, but her opponent's incessant little pointers on the 'western grip' had simply grown too odious). Eric had vaulted over the sagging fence into her court and proposed cockily, 'How about a real game?' He might have been intrigued already, but it was only after Willy slaughtered Eric himself that her new admirer fell in love. In retrospect, he seemed captivated initially less by Willy the woman than by the fact that she beat the pants off him. Willy sometimes entertained the nauseous suspicion that, had she been off-form that afternoon and lost their original head-to-head, she and Eric would never have married.

Throughout their courtship as well, Willy's superior prowess on the baseline had kept Eric coming back for more. You didn't tempt Eric Oberdorf with a pretty dress, but with a slinky down-the-line slice that played hard-to-get. With her two extra years on the circuit, Willy's subtle touch and cunning got the better of her neophyte boyfriend every time. Still, she could locate a trace anxiety even in those heady days of her confident and considerable pre-eminence. The onus to win once was a challenge, to which Willy rose with appetite. The obligation to win all the time was a burden. And over the long haul, certain crude facts would inevitably factor in: that Willy was only five-three, while Eric was a full foot taller; and that Willy, however resentfully, was a girl.

Consequently, whenever Eric acclaimed the genius of his newest acquisition, Willy ground her teeth. He may as well have drooled over some other woman's sexy gams and pert breasts. That her promiscuous husband's practice opponents were male merely brought Willy's jealousy to a boil. Only men could feed Eric the pace he craved; only men could dish out serves at 120mph. Willy couldn't compete.

At least in the public sphere Willy had retained an edge. When they met, Willy was ranked 437; Eric had barely eked onto the ATP computer, stranded in the late 900s. With such a drastic disparity, Willy had felt safe. The hundreds of digits acted like a mote – if she was reluctant to name just what they protected her from. Yet since their marriage nearly a year ago, Eric had closed this gap improbably, thinning what began as a vast sea of achievement between them to a river narrow enough for him to wave cheerfully from the opposite shore. Willy herself had made stolid progress, improving her ranking to 289, but while she was hefting steadily up the ladder Eric had been bounding two rungs at a time: after a mere eighteen months playing satellite tournaments, her husband had clambered to 517. Eric was swiftly growing into his game, much the way a lanky adolescent discovers that his father's jacket, which drowned him the year before, is this year a snug fit.

Against all odds, Eric had yet to defeat his wily, agile wife. But the happy massacre of their first face-off was now far from standard. Nowadays they always went three sets; tie-breaks were frequent; games went to deuce.

The tactics to which Willy was forced to stoop were fiendish. Besides, with his gluttonous taste for fresh meat, Eric and Willy had played each other no more than once every six weeks. Since for months she'd beaten him by a hair's breadth,

Willy had suffered the growing unease through that autumn that in this infrequency was reprieve.

On their first anniversary, however, Eric cleared his calendar for a ceremonial re-match. December dictated an indoor date at the Upper West Side's Hamilton Jordan Racquet Club, where they held a family membership. As she strode to the net post at the same time of day that they'd wed, Willy's hands buzzed with the tremble that ordinarily signalled the onset of a vital finals match. When she peeled the flip-top, a rubbery breath exhaled from the Wilson can. Commonly the perfume of opportunity, just this afternoon the smell was spiked with an acrid tinge.

The same sharp, acid scent exuded from Eric's new togs, fresh from the package – his Lycra cross-training shorts, cotton over-shorts, and roomy designer sports shirt were all solid black. As Willy had worn her plain white tournament dress, the aesthetic of the classic western prevailed. A triangulated black bandanna obscured his receding hairline, Eric's sole physical flaw. When he smiled, his teeth, under artificial lighting, flashed little knives.

In the warm-up, rather than keep the ball in play to groove their strokes, Eric continually put the ball away. If Willy initiated a rally with an easy mid-court forehand, Eric cracked his return to skid the alley-line, and Willy would trudge to fetch the ball. He hurried the racket flip for serve, though Willy had not remotely hit her stride.

Leaning forward to receive, twirling his racket, rocking side to side, Eric had the shiny eyes, tensed muscles, and spittle-flecked mouth of a hound with the hare in sight. Willy bounced the ball, unable to put her finger on why something felt wrong. The toss was a little low, and as she wound up at its crest Willy identified the disconcerting sensation – one which afflicted Willy, despite the bald black-and-white description on her passport, seldom.

She felt short.

Her double-fault was inauspicious. Eric trotted to the ad-court, leered forward again, juggling his grip. He *broke her* the first game, and today the expression was resonant.

'Do you have to chew gum?' Willy implored on the change-over.

'I always chew gum', Eric smacked.

'It's obnoxious'.

'It's supposed to be'. He blew a bubble, and popped it with a relish that usually comes with bursting someone else's.

Her trouble was sourced in the preliminaries, which Eric had truncated to five minutes. Eric could switch his game on like a radio. But Willy's strokes didn't sing instantaneously. Until a melody gathered in her body, the racket felt clunky, apart.

Eric was so eager to punish the ball into oblivion that their rallies were rare. The fits and starts of first few games had no music. Willy had gone down in the first set 4–6 before the object in her right hand felt like a racket and not like a shovel.

Between sets they toweled down. 'Of course, you *know* I need fifteen minutes to find my game', she said. 'I've even told you'.

'No need', said Eric. 'I've seen it. In a quarter of an hour, you improve by a factor of five'.

'On the stock exchange, you'd be arrested', she sniped, marching off to serve. 'It's called 'insider trading'.'

Her husband's retort boomed off the high ceiling, 'It's called marriage!'

In the second set, Eric's renowned on-court relaxation took a twist toward the snide. As he sauntered back and forth to receive, he took his time. His commonly erect posture was compromised by a contemptuous slouch. Picking up balls, he flipped the Wilson with the tip of his frame, then ponged it off the strings with a twirl between bounces, as if he needed some extra amusement to keep himself entertained. Smacking gum on the baseline, he looked more like a street-corner tough than a pro tennis player.

While Eric pursued his usual policy of saying nothing, there was a new development: every time he missed a shot, no matter how taxing, he laughed – as if muffing such a piece of cake were hilarious.

Willy's forehead began to pinch with an ominous headache. Anger in sports ran all the risks of nuclear power. Before her building fury blew up in her face, she had to harness and channel it, to wire her wrath to the ball. On the other hand, no matter how much weight she threw behind her shots, that was never more than 108 pounds. Eric was used to playing other men; no amount of feminine zing fazed him. Willy could hit a heavy ball, for a woman. But in male terms, her pace was no better than respectable.

It was crucial not to be lured into playing his game. She would never overpower him. So Willy switched to cold fusion. Though it was gratifying in the moment to fry the ball, the only enduring satisfaction was to win. At 4–4, she dialed back the voltage, playing percentages, opting more to press than to destroy.

Though this cagey hunkering down elicited multiple chortles from her husband, she could still do no better than hold serve, and likewise in the tie break. Impatient with a tit for tat that at $65/hour could last from now till doomsday, Willy saw her chance and threw her switches. Instead of sending his deep lob to her backhand safely down the line, Willy ran around to her forehand for an inside-out overhead. That left the rest of the court for the taking; if he hauled ass to return, she was dead. Her coach would have turned purple.

As it happened, the overhead did clear the tape by the requisite half inch and nicked the line. Eric was nowhere nearby, but back on his baseline chewing gum, adjusting his black kerchief at a jaunty angle. Propped against his knee, his racket was not even in his hand. 'Touché', he said, with an indulgent smile, as if she had just done something cute.

It may be no coincidence that there are both three sets in the dynamic tennis match and three acts in the classical play. Each set completes a discrete sub-drama, whose intricate ins and outs can distract from the larger story. Hence Willy's triumph in taking the second set was quickly washed away in the briefest of intermissions, after which the players took their places. Dramatically, at 1–1 there is no telling whether the second set represents a turned tide, or a red herring.

In the first two sets what had got Willy's goat was Eric's apparent leisure – his insolent, ball-bobbling nonchalance, the sort of hip, slovenly posturing that most people could only manage with a cigarette. What dismayed her in the third was his exertion. Eric sloughed off his disguise of so-fucking-what to reveal how fantastically hard he was trying. He leapt two feet in the air to intersect a damned good lob; he never once conceded that her volley was too sharp to chase down, and surely he risked injury in some of the heaving changes of direction that his incredible retrievals demanded. Lunging for passing shots, he threw his whole body as if rescuing a wayward toddler from an oncoming bus. Of course she wanted him to make an effort; lack of application was an insult. But somehow he was going too far. He let her have nothing. He was even willing to hurt himself if that's what grappling a single point from her clutches cost him. Frankly, in none of the tournaments she'd watched him play had Eric put himself out quite so extremely as in trying to sandbag his own wife on their wedding anniversary.

And he had memorized her game like a poem. No matter what she hit, he seemed to know before the ball left her racket precisely where it was headed. Even when she aimed deliberately to surprise, he looked like a sneaky child who had peeked inside his Christmas package and failed to feign delight on opening it a second time.

Worse still, Willy kept recognizing her own esoteric shots, retooled and refurbished. Of course she didn't *own* the slice-drop, barely clearing the tape like a pole-vaulter grazing his back on the bar. Still Willy felt robbed when Eric duplicated her trademark, and not only reproduced but improved upon it, the way the Japanese manufacture an American car: one of Eric's slices had so much underspin that it somersaulted back to his own court. All her helpful hints of the preceding year Eric had faithfully installed, and Willy resented how kleptomaniacally Eric had *taken* her advice. When they met his game was scrappy; now that she'd shared her professional secrets only to have them used against her, she wanted them back. Surely usurping so many monogrammed shots wholesale was as unseemly as dressing up in her clothes.

A year before Eric's strokes were potent, but his strategy was predictable. Now between his blasting masculine drives he slyly interwove the female cunning of impetuous dinks, neurotic spins, and last-minute improvisations, when it was conventionally the prerogative of women to change their minds. Yet these feminine wiles were grafted to male muscle. The result was a game that glimmered with sexual ambiguity, like a construction worker with a few incongruously effeminate mannerisms, whose buddies can never quite decide if he's gay.

Willy could not even console herself that her own game was crumbling in return. Eric was hitting so fabulously well that he lifted her with him. Though her tactics were increasingly defensive, these were still very effective tactics. Rather than be disgusted with herself, in the main of the third set at 2–3 Willy considered that she may have been playing, wastefully, the best tennis of her life.

Best wasn't good enough.

Unlike the fits and starts of the first set, now their points were drawn out; every game went to deuce. But Willy's anger was spent. Try as she might, she couldn't despise him. As an aficionado of elegant tennis, Willy couldn't revile an artist on the court. Her dark, dashing husband himself looked only more exquisite, and his beauty was murderous.

At 4–2, Willy's arms went limp. Eric served to her ad-court. She didn't feint in the ball's direction, but allowed his ace to burst splendidly undefaced to the netting. She smiled, weakly, conceding with a quaver, 'Terrific serve'.

This and the final game were tribute. If Eric wanted her soul he could have it, though it grieved her that more than she could say that's what he craved: her dignity like a lamb on an altar. On match point she deliberately popped him a sitter, that he could fall upon it to his greater glory, and watched, sacrificial, as the ball hurtled from his overhead. Transfixed, she didn't realize it was rocketing straight for her until it clocked her on the breast.

He ran over. 'Are you all right?'

'Since when did you worry how I was?'

'Honey –' He touched her cheek.

She brushed him away. 'Happy?'

Eric shrugged.

'No, tell me. Are you *happy*? You got what you wanted. You won. It's our anniversary. Have I made your day?'

'Sweetheart, you've been pasting me for over a year. And somebody has to win, don't they?'

In her own mind, Willy had not been 'pasting' him; she'd won nothing but delay. Willy shoved her racket in its case; the zipper stuck. She wasn't furious. She was doleful. Something more than a tennis match had been lost. 'Congratulations', she mumbled. 'No one could say that you didn't put your whole heart into it'.

He touched her sleeve. 'Aren't you glad that I regard being able to best you once in a while as an achievement?'

Once in a while was false modesty. None of his other partners had ever broken back. Eric would see to it that she never outplayed him again.

Through the funereal unwinding of her bandanna, Eric pressed, 'You wouldn't want me to *let* you win, would you?'

'Of course not', she answered brusquely, but something bruised and girlish in her whispered, hissing, *Yesss.*

Lionel Shriver was born in North Carolina in 1957. She is the author of seven novels and has written extensively for *The Guardian*, *Wall Street Journal* and *The Economist*. She is also a regular panellist on BBC2's *Newsweek Review*. This is an excerpt from her latest book, *Double Fault* (Serpent's Tail, 2006), the follow-up to the hugely successful *We Need to Talk About Kevin* which won the Orange Prize for Fiction in 2005. She lives in London.

Willy Vlautin

Kid Collins

Walt Collins is at the Fitzgerald playing Twenty One when his sister, Lorna, waves to him from across the table. She has her five year old daughter Cora with her. She also has a black eye and a line of dried mascara down her cheek. She's wearing a blue dress with black shoes and holding her daughter's hand.

Walt pulls out of the game and walks to them and the little girl looks at him and he smiles and says hello. He looks at his sister.

'Are you alright?' he says. 'I haven't seen you in what six months? I don't even know where you live anymore. I stopped by a month ago but some old man had moved in there and said he'd been there six weeks'.

'Sorry Walt', she says, 'what are you doing here? I thought you said you quit? I've looked everywhere, this was my last stop'.

'I don't know what I'm doing', he says and looks around. 'What happened to your eye?'

'I need to talk to you about that', she said.

'Why did you bring her here?'

The small girl's staring into the crowded room watching people walk past her. Her shoes are untied. She's wearing green shorts and a yellow T-shirt. Her knees are muddy. Her arms are covered in dirt, grease.

'How you doing kid?' Walt says and pats her on the head.

'Okay', the girl says.

'Kid Collins', he says and drops down to his knees.

'You gonna give your uncle a hug?'

The girl goes to him and hugs him.

'You still gonna be a boxer?'

The girl nods her head.

'Kid Collins. The southpaw from Reno, Nevada'.

Lorna's hands are twitching. She can't stand still. 'Walt', she says, 'I need to talk to you. It's important. You know I'd never ask for anything'.

'Alright', Walt says and stands up. 'But let's get the hell out of here. I don't think Cora can be in here and my stomach's starting. I got to get some pepto. You still got a car?'

'Yeah'.

'I don't anymore', he says and tries to smile.

'Where you want to go?'

'Let's take the kid to Gold 'N Silver'.

Walt kneels down again.

'You want to get something to eat, Kid?'

'Yes', the girl says.

'You know your mom and me, we used to eat at the Gold 'N Silver when we were kids. Our folks would take us every Saturday until we were at least in high-school'.

'Let's go', Lorna says, 'I'm serious'.

'I'm as good as done here anyway', he says and stands. 'I got to cash out. Where you parked?'

'At Molly Malones', she says.

'What kind of car you got?'

'A 1983 Honda Civic. It's silver. I'll wait for you there'.

'It won't take me long', he says and heads back to the table.

They park in the back lot of the Gold 'N Silver.

Walt gets out and lights a cigarette.

'Stay in the car honey', Lorna says, 'I have to talk to your Uncle Walt. I'll bring you out a grilled cheese. Does that sound good?'

'Yes', the girl says.

'I love you', Lorna says. 'You know that, don't you?'

'Yes', the little girl says.

She kisses her daughter then shuts the car door and locks it.

Walt's standing on the sidewalk smoking.

'Let her come in. You can't just leave her here'.

'I'll get her something', Lorna says, 'anyway I just need to talk for a bit. I can't stay long'.

'Suit yourself', Walt says and drops the cigarette to the ground and stomps on it with his foot. 'We'll be right back, Kid. You just hang tight', he says and waves to her, then turns around and follows his sister inside the building.

They sit at a booth and Lorna orders coffee and Walt orders a large glass of milk and a side order of white toast.

'First things first', she says as the waitress leaves, 'I got to tell you, I love you, Walt. You've always been good to me'.

'Well Lorna, Jesus, what's going on?'

'I don't know where to begin', she says and begins crying.

'Are you in some sort of trouble?'

'I think I am', she says and wipes her tears with a napkin. 'Are you still gambling?'

'I'm trying not too. Something's wrong with my stomach. The doctor says I have to quit drinking. I don't mind, though. I'm tired of it. Tired of gambling too. I slip up once in awhile but I'm almost there'

'Are you working?'

'I'm selling cars', he says and laughs.

'Jesus', Lorna says and smiles. 'I haven't worked since the last time I saw you. I'm a fucking mess, Walt'.

'I've seen you look better', he says.

'Thanks', she says.

'You still doing that stuff?'

'Some', she says.

'What do you need from me?'

'Just to talk to me for a little bit'.

'How's Cora?'

'She's a sweet heart', Lorna says and begins to cry again. 'I ain't been much of a mother'.

'What do you mean?'

'We just been living at people's houses. I don't even have an apartment. I've left her with some terrible people'.

'You can stay with me', Walt says. 'It ain't much. I'm just renting a room at the El Cortez, but it's something'.

'I think we're gonna have to leave town'.

'Where are you gonna go?'

'I don't know, maybe Arizona. I have a girlfriend down there'.

'Is Cora in school?'

'She's just turned five'.

'When they start school?'

'Six, first grade starts when you're six'.

'Is it the best thing for you, to move to Arizona?'

'I think so, yes', she says and looks in her purse. 'I've owed you a lot of money over the years, Walt, haven't I?'

'You don't have to worry about that right now', he says.

'Just take this. Money's the least of my problems', she says and takes an envelope from her purse. She lays it onto the table. 'There's what? Something like eighty dollars here. I want you to take it'.

'I don't need your money', Walt says.

'You might', she said. 'It'll make me feel better. It'll make me feel like a better person if you take it'.

'Look, Lorna just calm down and we'll figure out what to do. You just have to tell me what's going on'.

'What kind of place is the El Cortez?'

'It's the hotel on Second Street. When we were kids we used to eat there. At Fongs'.

'The Chinese restaurant?'

'That's the place'.

'I remember it now'.

'I'm on the fourth floor. I'll be out soon, though. It's just football, it about killed me this year so I lost my place and had to move in there. But I'm alright. Been going to meetings. I almost have it licked. Anyway, there's a bath and shower. There's a TV and a sink and a small fridge. I could get a pull-out bed for Cora and we could share the double bed until you get settled'.

'Is it safe for Cora?'

'It'll be alright for awhile. Nothing but old men mostly. I wouldn't want her there by herself. But with one of us around it'd be alright. I'll be out of there at the end of the month anyway. I've been doing good at the lot'.

'I'm sorry I'm such a wreck', she says.

'You got nothing to be sorry about. I've just worried about you. I kept trying to call you, but you never returned my calls and then it was disconnected'.

'I'm just so sorry', she says.

'What's going on?'

'I don't know', she says. 'I must look a mess'.

'You might want to wash your face. Your eye makeup's run all over'.

'Maybe I should clean up. I'll be right back. Remember to order Cora a grilled cheese. Get extra pickles too. I hope you don't hate me. You've always been so good to me'.

She grabs his hand then gets out of the booth and turns and disappears down the aisle towards the bathroom.

He waits nearly a half hour and drinks his milk and eats the toast. He gets up and goes to the women's room and calls for her inside. He sticks his head in, but it's empty, there's no one. He goes back to the table and pays the bill, takes the money she left and the sack with the grilled cheese and leaves.

He goes out the side entrance and looks in the parking lot for her car, but it isn't there. He thinks about taking a cab, but his stomach starts up and he thinks walking might somehow ease it. But soon he begins coughing up the milk and toast. He stops and vomits, walks another block, and then sits down on the sidewalk and wipes his face with his handkerchief. It's then that he notices the noise, the dragging noise. He looks up and in the dim light he sees the girl, Cora, dragging a suitcase by a piece of rope towards him.

'What you up to Kid?' he says and coughs as she nears him.

'I'm supposed to go with you', she says and stands in front of him.

'I didn't see you in the parking lot. Where were you?'

'Hiding in the bushes. I got scared'.

'That's a big suitcase, how'd you'd drag it all this way?'

'I have the rope', she says and smiles.

'Why don't you sit down and take a breather', he says, 'I got you a grilled cheese and fries'.

The girl sits next to him.

'What do you feel like doing after you eat?'

'TV', the girl says.

'That, Kid Collins, I can do', he says and hands her the bag.

Willy Vlautin was born in Reno, Nevada in 1967 and he currently lives in Portland, Oregan. He studied writing with the great Nevadan author Randell Reed, and has published short stories in magazines such as *Story* and *Zembla*. He is the songwriter and vocalist for the internationally acclaimed band, Richmond Fontaine, whose most recent album, *The Fitzgerald* (2005) was described by Q as 'the most beautiful sad album of the year'. His first novel, *The Motel Life*, is published by Faber and Faber in April 2006.

CLARE AZZOPARDI

The Green Line

Translated from Maltese by Albert Gatt

She has to get on.

Her brother and sister have made up their minds, she has no say in the matter. Stepney Green to London Victoria on the District Line. And bussing it is out of the question, because her brother's never been on the tube and the idea turns him on. As for her sister, an hour on the bus doesn't appeal to her because there's so much she wants to see and so little time.

If you've been fighting cancer for eighteen months and have spent days on end hooked up to a bag of chemotherapy watching vein after vein wither and die, nothing frightens you so much anymore. Likewise, if your husband left you for another man, and the boyfriend you've been seeing for just a few months takes his own life when he finds out about your husband and his boyfriend, nothing frightens you so much anymore.

Her brother's 24 and was diagnosed with lymphoma. Her sister's thirty; her marriage broke up after three years, and the first man she started dating after that left her a suicide note a month ago, in which he cited her as the reason.

So they've both made it amply clear. Death doesn't scare them. Given the choice, it's better to die in a terrorist attack than pine away from depression or cancer. She thinks differently. Her legs feel numb as she descends into Stepney station, and the whiplash of tail wind across her face makes her feel sick. And then she's on the train with her sister and her brother.

The train is completely deserted.

Everybody else is still under shock after the events of a couple of days ago, with the exception of her siblings, whose orders she feels she has to follow, although quite frankly, this whole who-gives-a-fuck-about-death-and-dying thing is getting to her – dying is a serious business as far as she's concerned and let's face it, the prospect is pretty distant, probably further away than the last stop on the green line.

The other thing is, her brother and sister want to play the part of the tourists to the hilt. She doesn't. The last time she was in London she was studying here, so she didn't qualify as a tourist. The last time she was in London, she'd decided she wanted to move here for a few years because she loved the city, it didn't put her to sleep despite the darkness which seeped into her veins. In fact, the city usually gave her the energy she now lacked because her brother and sister had squeezed it out of her, down to the last drop. She'd been the one to encourage them to make the trip in the first place.

Idiot.

And suddenly, London just isn't the same anymore.

Whitechapel.

Her brother glances at the tube map. *Eleven more stops to go,* he says.

Having made up her mind that she hasn't got much longer to live, she begins to think of all the things she would like to have asked her father, things she'd never managed to extract from him.

- do you remember the time we used to go down to the playing field and there'd be this box of canned foodstuffs on that old woman's doorstep?

- no, not really.

- what was her name?

- don't remember.

- you can't not remember, I was with you a couple of times and you told me not to mention it to anyone.

- so you shouldn't be talking to me about it either.

- and you parked some distance away and ran to get the box, dumped it in the boot, and then we were off again.

- no, don't remember.

- and what about the time I started crying in the morning because I wanted to go to school and you said I couldn't...?

- no, you never cried.

- 'course I did, and then you were saying that school was out and we were on holiday. And I'd seen the boy from next door go to school, so why couldn't I ...

- that was a long time ago.

- but you do remember that you went on strike don't you!?

- I'd forget about that too if I could.

- and do you remember how we used to go to the port in Valletta to wait for Pantu to come back from Gozo carrying the boxes of veg that nann Roza would send?

- What are you talking about?

- don't you remember anything anymore?

- and what about the time nannu got us our first colour tv?

- can't say I remember.

- of course, we were the only ones in the family not to have one.

- you're mixing things up.

- did your going on strike have something to do with it?

- no.

- and the fact that nannu worked at the dockyard, did that have something to do with it?

- no.

- and nannu'd got them all on the black market, or for free, even.

- ask him.

- he got one for himself first, and then one for aunt Jenny, and then it was uncle Manuel and finally we got one of our own.

- I don't remember.

- so why did you accept it anyway?

Tower Hill.

This friend of hers who's getting married soon is afraid of going on a honeymoon to Tuscany. Apparently, at the same time that he and his wife were planning to go, Tony Blair will be in Tuscany, which according to some makes it the next likely target. And this other friend of hers, a German, she's lived in London for a long time and says she'd never missed a day's work until that day, when she woke up feeling queasy and phoned in sick. And she suddenly thinks of Marthese, who also used to live in London but with whom she's lost contact after a tiff they had in Republic Street, when Marthese had said she was selfish and she'd called Marthese a coward, at which point Marthese took off her top and bra in full view of everyone, just to prove that she wasn't. And though she'd have liked to do something to prove that she wasn't selfish, she didn't. So she's wondering now whether Marthese also called in sick that morning.

And then she looks at her sister, stares into the turmoil in her eyes, is on the verge of telling her that now is their last chance to talk over all the things that need to be cleared up, seeing as they're about to die. Her sister seems to understand, but it's so quiet on the train she picks up a book instead. One of those awful paperbacks, which is all she seems to read.

- do you remember playing doctor and patient when we were kids, and I'd always tell you to get undressed (though I was the younger), and I'd give you a full examination as you lay stark naked, top to toe, with my apron on?

No, she doesn't remember.

- you used to enjoy it too.

She doesn't remember.

- and do you remember how, on your wedding day, just before we went into church wearing our best smiles, you told me you didn't love this man and that this was going to be the biggest mistake of your life? And I gave you a dirty look.

She doesn't remember that either.

- and what about when I told you I prefer women to men, in fact I find men disgusting? You just changed the subject.

Nope, she can't remember.

Her sister chuckles at a bad joke in the book.

Monument.

This other friend of hers likes to compare her life to the London tube map. It veers off in all sorts of directions, each one with a clear starting point and destination, and you knew the time of departure and the duration. The tube colours stood for her (many) moodswings. And the (even more numerous) stops were the relationships she walked into depending on which mood she was in, involving different people on different routes. Right now she's wishing she could ask her friend about her contingency plan for when parts of the underground have to be shut down because somebody's planted a bomb. Her friend once told her that during a visit to London she'd spent all of her time on the underground. The idea of being able to visit every point on the map with a single ticket appealed to her. She'd get off the train at every stop and then catch the next one out to her next destination, marking every stop she'd been to on the map in pencil. By the time she had them all marked, it was time to go back to Malta.

Blackfriars.

Someone gets on the train, and he's carrying a backpack. She hates herself for being prejudiced but can't really help it, her mind seems to race on ahead oblivious. It thinks its thoughts and concludes that panic is warranted. But what she really can't get her head around is how someone with a family and a decent job could decide to blow himself to pieces and kill some forty others in the process. And how this someone could decide that she was going to die along with him.

Her throat feels constricted. Glancing down into the crypt of her mind, her brother seems to notice. She's about to tell him that since they won't be alive for much longer, now might be a good time to go over that day when he'd thrown the pointed kitchen knife at her during an argument. She tries to remind him by staring flick-knives into his eyes.

- do you remember when you threw that knife at me and missed me by a hair's breadth?

He can't remember.

- and I picked it up and was on the verge of throwing it right back at you, then I went out and scratched the side of your new car instead.

He doesn't remember.

- it might be a good idea to apologise, we're going to die pretty soon anyway.

He's not paying attention.

- and do you remember the time when the oncologist told you you had a tumour? And then the next doctor you visited, and the one after that, both said it wasn't a tumour at all, just a hernia, and that evening you were telling me about it and we were both in fits, and when you blacked out I simply kept on laughing 'cause I thought it was all part of the act. And then you didn't get up and we rushed you to hospital. And we left the hospital without you.

But he's still counting the remaining stops to London Victoria.

It turned out not to be a tumour in the end. It wasn't a hernia either, though.

Temple.

Then there's this paranoid friend of hers who's always convinced that someone's going to break into her flat during the night. Not that she's afraid of being raped or anything like that, she's convinced that it's her laptop they'll be after. Her laptop contains the beginning of a novel she's been hacking away at for six years. So her friend saves the novel every Saturday morning (thieves tend to pay their visits on a Saturday night) and hides the CDs in different parts of her flat. She used to find her friend's behaviour hilarious, but now she's the one who's in the grip of paranoid thoughts, making the sign of the cross every time a bearded man with a backpack gets on the train.

She takes her mobile phone out of her handbag and starts writing a text to her friend.

i'll give u a hand with d Lowell
thing when I get back. we'll
cook sth up. if I die spare a thought
for us gal

Now she's started to generalise in just the way she hates, go figure. But suddenly she feels an urge to bump this Lowell guy off, 'cause he's a fascist who's sworn to kill all the *klandestini* that make it to Malta.

The bastard.

Turns out there's no network down here, so she saves the text to send later. That's assuming she'll have made it through.

Embankment.

Why is it, she starts to think, that when someone is pissed off, he can't just lock himself up in the toilet and scream his heart out, instead of bumping himself and about fifty other people off. That's what she does, for example, whenever her mother starts gabbing about premarital sex, or her father asks her on a Sunday morning whether she's been to church. At this point, she shuts her eyes and thinks of her mother and of the last row they had, and feels a strong urge to tell her that finally she's going to be rid of her once and for all, because this is it, her daughter's going to die, so she won't have to worry anymore about what the neighbours think of her daughter. She'd also like to ask her about aunt Cetta, as she always does, just to try and get her to talk straight for once.

- so what's with aunt Cett and Pina?

- what about them?

- christ, they're inseparable!

- right.

- Oh come on, ma, doesn't everybody know that your sister and her friend are always sticking together!

- I've no idea what you're on about.

- well, stands to reason ...

- what?

- it's all inherited down your side of the family!

- what is?

- nanna's sister was like that too ... only they had her down as an old spinster

- I can't remember.

- funny, that, 'cause I certainly remember.

- how could you remember? You were six when my mother's sister passed away!

- She had a girlfriend too. Ganna, I even remember her name, she was always talking about her.

- I simply don't remember.

- and now Pina's started to sleep over at aunt Cett's.

- what's that got to do with anything?

- 'course it does.

- she's sick isn't she? She needs someone to take care of her.

- you know, you're so gullible, you'll buy anything, even from a couple of sixty year-olds.

- you keep going on about this.
- you never admit it.
- admit what?
- that's why you'll never understand.
- I still have no idea what you're on about.
- that's 'cause it suits you better not to know.
- know what?
- let's face it, this business with aunt Cett and Pina ...
- yes ...
- there's no way I've got that wrong.
- it's not important.
- aren't I important?
- we've got enough on our plate as it is.
- but that's just it, this isn't a problem...

This morning her cousin told her he'd like to sit in the underground playing the guitar sometime, not really for the money, just to try it out, see whether anyone would stop and listen, whether they'd like the songs he writes. Her cousin lives in Stepney Green and calls himself a Londoner. He insists that he wouldn't want to live anywhere else, despite the racist remarks that people occasionally pass when he gets on the bus. He says that although he isn't blond and good-looking, he's made up his mind to stay put, because, rundown as this place may be, it's still his birthplace. And he says that whenever something is bothering him, music is all he needs, so he's made up his mind that now's the time to carry out his plan to play in the underground, just to make the point that he isn't scared. Then he asked her whether she'd spare a little change if she was ever passing through and came across him playing, at which point she just lost it and chucked a shoe at him in reply.

Westminster.

It's stifling in here. There's a smell she can't identify; the sensation in her sinus reminds her of Duncan's fingers up her nostrils the day they had a row over a bit of weed. She can almost feel the blood trickle down as it did that time. The wobbly feeling in her legs reminds her of that evening spent on Hastings Bastions with her shoes in her lap and her legs jutting off the edge, catching the cool breeze. It wasn't long before she'd started crying though. Then she'd lit a cigarette and repeatedly stubbed it on her flabby thighs. It hurt. Which again brings these people to mind, who take it into their heads to become suicide bombers. Why don't they lay into themselves with a blade until the pain becomes unbearable, as she does whenever she feels angry at the whole world, feels like taking it out on the whole of humanity. Another thing they could do is light a fag and stub it out on their eyelids, it's a pretty effective reminder of how much burning hurts. That's what she does when everything and everyone seems to have it in for her. But to just bump yourself off, not to mention a whole lot of other people, jesus fucking christ that's... just not on, ever. She knows, she's tried it several times and has never managed to go through with it. Hurting yourself when you were pissed off she can understand, though. It works too.

She glances once more at her brother. *We'll be there soon,* he says. She feels the urge to tell him that she loves him, and wouldn't want him to die even though they have these nasty rows and he calls her a git because she can't seem to hold down a job for longer than three months. Then he tells her she should consider becoming a train driver 'cause it seems to be an easy and fun kind of job, she might even manage to stick it out for longer than three months. So she aims a kick at him. What she's dying to tell him is that they should probably start taking life a little more seriously, stop taking the piss out of each other, because they were about to die.

Victoria Station.

A desert.

This is the first time she's seen that station in such a desolate state, waiting for the people to turn up, sending off train after empty train, forlorn in the absence of the morning rush ... what is she doing here? She needs to look happy because this is the first time her brother's been underground. Her sister looks as if she's standing on the cusp of the new world. She herself used to feel that way when she was in London, except that now everything seems to have died, and she's even begun to consider the possibility that maybe this isn't the best place to spend the rest of one's life after all. Then she sees the policemen with their dogs. Shortly after, a man in civvies walks past carrying a squarish brown briefcase, looking as though he's searching for explosives. Her brother finds this really cool and takes a picture of him. She feels a strong urge to shove her head into a dustbin and feel sick, but there are no dustbins in Victoria, and it's probably not such a good idea to make a mess on the station floor.

This friend of hers wakes up at 5 am on the dot every morning and eats 100g of Special K, then goes right back to bed and sleeps until six thirty, when she gets up and heads straight for the loo. Her friend is convinced that this routine makes her life so much easier compared to other people who don't get up before eight and then have to rush to be at work by eight thirty. So one day she asked her friend what would happen if she didn't hear the alarm clock ringing, but her friend assured her that this eventuality had never occurred, so she asked her friend what would happen if she woke up to find that she'd run out of Special K, but her friend assured her that this eventuality had never occurred either. If she could, she'd ask her friend now what she'd do if she found herself on an exploding train and was taken to a hospital where they simply didn't serve Special K at five am and, moreover, going to the loo at six thirty was out of the question. But her friend is probably too laid back to even think about things that don't concern her directly, which is probably why her life is so much easier, and she wishes she could be like that herself, but just can't see herself waking up to a bowl of Special K at five in the morning. She'd be sick of the stuff after a week anyway.

Meanwhile, her brother and sister have been looking up the route to Leicester Square. The Piccadilly Line. Part of it has been shut down, but they can still catch a train to Leicester. She's feeling dizzy and her legs seem to be made of lead. She just can't face another ride on the tube. Why not take a walk? It's not such a great distance. The police are still sniffing around with their dogs. The man with the briefcase is still around too. Her brother and sister take off in the direction of the Piccadilly Line. She starts to have visions of her friend eating her Special K, her cousin strumming *Julia* somewhere in the underground, her mother praying, her father muttering the rosary, her friend staring at the tube map, the bearded man getting on the train, her brother at Boffa Hospital, her sister in bed all alone. She needs to feel the chill of the ground beneath her feet, so she takes of her shoes and socks, rolls up her jeans, and walks barefoot.

She gets home and shuts the door behind her, turns the keys in both the top and bottom locks, slides the bolt home on the side window, and stumbles the last few steps into her bedroom. She draws the nylon curtain, then the drapes with their stripey pattern. The light outside is as irksome as the repetitive yammering from a scratched CD. She takes off her belt, undoes the button of her trousers and unzips it with some difficulty, releasing the flab on her stomach. She tears her shirt open with such livid force, the buttons come off and she hears them as they hit the floor: One, two, three, four. They remind her of the beads she used to play with when she was a little girl, of how, when she got tired of playing with them, she'd try to get the cat to swallow them to see her choke. She takes off her shirt, drops it behind her onto the bed. She pulls her trousers and panties down. First one leg, then the other. Unhooks her bra, lowers the strap over first one and then the other arm. She looks in the mirror. Grabs a bottle of perfume in her right hand, squeezes it tight between her fingers. Stares at it. She lifts her right arm, squeezes the bottle even harder. She draws herself back a little and ... screams.

Her body slams down hard onto the bed, she shuts her eyes.

Getting up after a few minutes, she stares once more into the mirror and is aware of a tear teetering over the edge of her eyelids, reluctant to take the plunge. She walks to the bathroom. Opens the door. Walks in. Shuts the door behind her. Turns the key, sits on the toilet and hugs the cistern, holding the handle of the flushing.

And she thinks of good sex. Of how she felt like throwing up after sleeping with Silvan that night. Of her mother, of every time she tells her *sleeping with a man is a sin, sleeping with a woman is three times as sinful.* And then, of her father, of when her father asks *Which Mass are you going to this morning?* She remembers her time in London with her brother and sister, how everything had happened at once and she'd felt like stubbing out a hundred cigarettes on her thighs, and had ended up walking barefoot through the station instead. And she wishes there was some way to ascertain that the bathroom is in fact the safest place to be.

With her arms around the cistern to keep her solitude at bay.

Clare Azzopardi is a writer and teacher from Malta. She has written and edited several publications for children and her poetry and short stories have appeared in several anthologies and magazines, including *In Focus* (the literary review of PEN Cyprus, 2005) and *Ktieb Ghall-Hruq* (Inizjamed, 2005). Her most recent publication is *Others, across,* an English translation of her short stories.

Oleh Lysheha

The Mind and the Hand

An Excerpt from *A Different Format*
with a preface note
Translated from Ukranian by
Oksana Tatsyak and James Brasfield

(In 2003, over a number of days Taras Prokhasko interviewed Oleh Lysheha, and from the recordings Prokhasko transcribed only Lysheha's responses to capture 'how Oleh Lysheha thinks aloud in everyday life'. The translated excerpt that follows is from the small book transcribed from the recordings, A Different Format.*)*

Some say that everything in nature is tamed. Maybe it is so. But I believe that we still preserve the idea of 'untameness' and that this concept of 'untameness' is complete and eternal. It differs much from the utilitarian concept of 'tameness'.

There is a concept of what remains wild. Well, it can also be considered from a social point of view; there is no way around that. But there is a different wildness – we look at a flower, and it's different. It is untamed. For this, there is no other concept.

We talk about the concept of tameness from a human point of view. That's right. That's how it is. But the earth is divided into the world of mankind and an entirely different world. Everything is dual: tamed or untamed. Perhaps there is such a dialectic: Existence consists of the great world of the tamed and the untamed. The world pulses-tick-tack, here and there ... and in this balance the poet sides with untamed nature which can always take an unexpected turn and renew the individual. All the rest pushes us into a cage. It is hard to define, but it seems to me that even my pottery becomes tamed. This is the thing. OK, my pottery is tamed, but everything depends on the hand that tamed it.

There are clouds. There is the earth which will never be tamed. How can you think that this great earth, believing that it is alive, is ...
One can say it is tamed, but the earth is a wild she-goat.

...

There is a concept of night, a concept of a different approach.

Is a man so self-confident that he thinks if I am fine today, I should be fine tomorrow? This is, of course, a great illusion. So who or what should we bow to? To that man who thinks we should be fine always? Yet always it should be different. Nature gives us a chance to be different, to discover happiness.
Who gives us the right to deprive nature of its divine qualities?

Nature is the same as God. If one believes that there is something out there, if one believes that there is the god who can turn things one way or another, then what follows? There is a continuation of God. This is not heathenism. It is eternity.

I don't know how one can live eternally in a predetermined world. If everything seems to exist already, then we find ourselves in a cage and our every step means nothing. We have entered a great negation if there is nothing that could be something else, nothing that might transform us.

We know that God is an eternity. Why is it so hard to believe?

...

It is not a question of whether it could be good here. What is deeper and what sustains life are entirely different matters. No one imposes anything here. There are mountains that tell you – you are here. There is a valley that tells you more. They will never tell me it's nicer here, or worse there. And there is fate. These are profound matters.

I can *see* mountains; I can dream of being in mountains, but I will never be there ... well, it won't work ... *yet I think about them*. This is fate.

In the valley I can feel liberated in the same way as in the mountains. I can feel liberated in the mountains and in the valley.

I can feel liberated, whether something is actually there or not. I can't say whether it is good that something is there or not. But I do think about this.

And it means that I am there ...

...

One cannot say that I am a man from Tysmenytsia; however, this is precisely where I am and this is a determinant.

For me the concept of the bear is important. For me, this is a creature, animal or man, that comprehends everything. But I did not see it here, in Tysmenytsia.

I would never wish for everything to be told in my name. Perhaps, rather by a

Cro-Magnon man. This is an interesting thing. No one can tell when he lived and where it was.

I wish there were nothing personal in all this, that one could speak neutrally, namelessly, so that it is not about a person because the person, for me, is frightening. Let's not talk about this. The view has to be abstract. Another matter is that this view has survived till our time, and it doesn't change – I mean the Cro-Magnon man. Though an abstraction, he burnt fires and did some kind of fishing. And all this continues up to now.

Our times created names. Somebody said this and somebody did that. It was all done ... done for the sake of the community. Always for the community. And always there was some kind of ruler who was overthrown or was not.

The concept of the poet's name appeared later. For us, perhaps, only with the arrival of Shevchenko, in the 19th century, the concept of the individual appears.

I wish that what is told were not told on behalf of the individual.
I wish that it were on behalf of a person from Tysmenytsia, or a Cro-Magnon man. It's a different matter that I would like to change my last name, that it were no more, but I've not found a new name.

I would like to see an evolution in thinking. [Ivan] Franko said, 'I am Franko'. He did say this and it is fine. But for me the person does not exist yet. It is not here yet. Did it happen? I am not interested in names. I am interested to see how it goes on and the names will come later. What are names? ...

Or what is the pride of kin? ...

Never. I will not have any part of it. Do you believe that such pride was built on moral acts? Pride must be anonymous. How can an oak, or poplar, or an ash tree be proud of kin? He can be proud. He can be proud that he survived great cataclysms. But should one be proud that he's better than his brethren?

What can the man of *belles-lettres* confirm? Who is better or who is worse? It is the way it is. There is a concept of great solidarity. And solidarity becomes great trees. This is the best thing that can happen. This is why I wanted to change my last name. It's unpleasant for me to show off one thing, or another. Well, fine. What is my kin? Well, some of my kinsmen were in different camps. There were some interesting representatives among them. But all this can be burnt in the fire of culture.

One has to deserve one's last name. Thus I would like to see a trace of anonymity through all these conversations. The idea of understanding. Thinking. This does not depend on the matter of names. If there is thinking ...

There is a person, and he can reveal himself through his thoughts. If there is no thinking, then the last name has no significance.

A stone reveals something of what it is, or it does not. It has to be anonymous.

...

I said something about the bear from the Spanish mountains.

This is a first manifestation of creativity. In Spain, perhaps they found a large boulder and covered it with a bear skin. Then they aimed at it. They aimed at it with round stones. And this is the first manifestation of art, art in a contemporary sense of the word. Aiming.

Afterwards, they moved the boulder toward a wall and created a relief of a bear. Then came a drawing of the bear, the profile. And then, then the presentation. But it all began with the intention to kill, or to be arrogant. Or maybe all is articulated as a means to possess.

The stones thrown were words. In one way or another, literature preserves the remnants of this magic – to aim. To aim at the most vulnerable points of the bear: the head, an eye. The bear survived, but is still aimed at with the precision of a sniper in a shooting gallery. One speaks of an archaic understanding when one comprehends the meaning of this later spiritual development.

The archaic understanding is to know what a branch is by pulling it closer to oneself and smelling it. There, one has an understanding. Such are the most ancient movements.

...

Fire. It's one of the most beautiful spectacles which leads to dependency. One can watch a fire over and over again – a fire which is under control – because there can be a fire which will not permit itself to be watched.

For a while I fired pottery in Kyiv. I had a very intense period of making pottery, around 1984. In the Vynohradari district of Kyiv there is a large pine forest (I found turtles there once). After woodsmen thinned the forests, there were huge branches between the pines. I had forgotten that such was done, but the wood was good. And beyond the forest was a valley, where I carried the half-rotten timber. In the evening I fired the pottery – five different pieces. It was winter and I began with a small fire made from weeds, to warm up the area. I placed the pottery, wrapped in kerchiefs, around the fire. The pieces became warm, then I put them into the ashes and covered them with weeds, then with sheet metal or an old bucket or basin. After they sat like this for an hour, I uncovered them, then covered them all with wood piled up like a mountain ... The mountain began humming and went on like that for five hours. I would look into the fire and see the pottery shining. When they were shining with a white glow, they were almost ready. Then gradually it was enough.

And when I returned home – around one or two in the morning – all scorched, covered with ashes, my eyelashes singed, I would see the fire in my dream. And this was frightening. I felt as if the dream were the fire, as if the flames not only fired my pottery but fired me as well from within. I was afraid, and from then on I knew that there are certain things in life through which you have to pass, as if through a tempering process; yes, you have to pass through fire. And this was already a conquered fire ...

But the fire at that place is an element. It's an element for the clay. The clay is so moldable, yet I don't know whether it wanted me to fire it. It passes through this metamorphosis. From a moldable feminine clay it transforms into a vessel that can satisfy both man and woman. This is a model of life.

Then I thought, was it worth it for me to go through this fire? It was worth it...if you sit in front of the fire for five hours, watching it burning and humming...I felt how it was firing something tender and childlike inside me. It is still burning.

Good, I thought, what about this clay? If using it only for paint, it stays raw. If I only paint with it, I simply use the clay, and there's no fire, so the clay doesn't pass through such an ordeal. I simply find it somewhere and it has different shades. And I realized that even this depends on my hands. Here are my hands ... Everything in art depends on the hand. The mind and the hand.

I trust the hand a lot. It is immediate. I thought if this is so, then the hand is the first to execute whatever is made. If I burn this hand, it's all over for me.

...

A man can express a movement with a gesture. When one hand joins the other and creates a chain, the hand expresses a movement. The hand essentially runs ahead of thoughts. But these are already subtleties...yet the hand leads, who knows, perhaps it leads the thought.

I feel that when I force myself to do the so-called mental work, nothing comes from it. On the other hand, when Nelia and I lived in Hlevakha and I wrote – always with the forest – I had to find the fallen pines that once grew in the forest. It was such a profound and essential movement. Nelia and I carried them on a sledge. It was a tremendous movement, more profound than that movement of the local train which runs everyday between Hlevakha and Kyiv, which signifies nothing. Afterwards we had to saw the wood, splinter it, burn it. And only then ... This was the particular movement connected to the fire. And there was also the connection with the fallen pines and with the forest. Such connections are not defined distinctly.

And there is the man in the city. Often his actions are chaotic. One depends on this or that; one needs this, this, and that. One doesn't consider the reason behind it (although there may be one).

But essentially the hand is connected to the movement. It's a powerful movement, not just a simple tick-tack movement. It is a movement of the elements. The hand remembers all this. I think it still carries memories from ancient times, though someone's hand may have greater memory than another's. Some people's movements become chaotic and less meaningful. Annulled. One may hold a cup, but not feel the curve of wood.

The movement is a logic that brings the wood into the fire.

Yet the wood does not have to be placed in the fire. Initially, a tree grows. Later, only the fallen tree can be burnt. Essentially the tree is something that rises and falls. A grand rhythm. And because the tree rises, a man must observe it. It's a kind of movement ... Not so different from a man who must grow up as himself.

...

I would like to tell you about my first fishing experience.

Now, I feel sorry for fish and I only look at them. In the US I caught a couple of fish and let them go. Whatever I catch with my hands seems to me that it is mine. But to catch anything in another way is over, not even catching fish with a pole. I've simply passed beyond the stage when I felt the excitement of a hunter, a natural born hunter or fisherman. It's over. But I do remember the smallest details of my childhood – my first fish, my first homemade fishing pole.

I found a stick and attached a thread to it. The hook was a staple, from a notebook, which I sharpened with a stone. That was it. And I walked carefree down the road from home, past a dam. There, the water was swirling and deep. As soon as I dropped the fishing line in, it pulled, bending the top of the stick –

the thread must have been quite strong, and when I saw the fish, it pulled me and I screamed, and ran for home, yelling, yelling. That was my first experience of the fish. At that moment I realized that the fish is a force of nature, a grand element. It's like water – after all, the fish lives right there. And it showed me what it was. I arrived at home all in tears, and only later did I come back to my senses.

But it was a big fish. It showed me what a fish is. Afterwards, there were other encounters. But this one was the beginning of something.

...

After the fourth grade, I wanted to enter the new art school in Tysmenytsia. I'd already done some drawing. My mother taught art and she heard that in order to be admitted, one had to show some preliminary work.

I remember the still life.

So my first still life was of a pottery jar (a glazed pitcher) with mushrooms around it. But the jar was placed upside-down. It was incredible ... It also testifies to a good start.

The jar was upside-down ... It was significant that it was upside-down. I don't know what it meant. And the mushrooms ... about a dozen white mushrooms someone had picked. It was just a still life. But there was so much in it – now I think of those mushrooms ...

The mushrooms are untamed nature. A jar is made by a hand. But they are connected, and there is nothing else.

Now these kinds of things are significant to me.

...

An interesting moment.

There are several archetypes in my life: a tree, a fire and clay. But they consist of finer ones. Their little brothers are also important. The archetypes – they are alive. I would never want them to become schemes. The archetypes should compliment one another. And the finer elements – branches or leaves – must be visible. That's what's interesting – how the images appear. How they appear together ... for me that is interesting. Perhaps I will never understand how they are born ... how their conversation is born. This also is an element, a grand element.

...

I called my book *To Snow and Fire.** If I've achieved something ample in this book, the space is important to me. Spiritual matters are immense. There is no pettiness in them. Perhaps, in human relationships there is pettiness sometimes and unnecessary things. But in the grand elements, there are no contingencies. There, everything is purposeful, especially form and colour.

The question arises again, What is primary? Is it form or colour? Or maybe a word? I want them to intermingle. I don't want to make conclusions about how it happened. That is unknown. The fact is that I was born, and already the word was here to find ... and I wanted to see what was primary. Because there was no hierarchy. It was all mutual. The elements were together. Always.

...

When you make a jar, you don't think how you will use it. Such an idea is unnecessary. Sooner or later, society makes commodities out of us. Even a person integrates into a society and one way or another becomes utilized. But I don't think about the jar's utility. I think about the pot as a creation of my hands. And at the same time, I believe that my hands have a great degree of wildness in them. The wildness of how it all came to be. I don't know. Perhaps it came to be out of hands which were not tamed. I believe they were not part of the cultural space, but a part of nature.

**To Snow and Fire*, a volume of poems, published 2002.

Oleh Lysheha was born in 1949 in western Ukraine. In 1972 he was expelled from Lviv University as a dissident. A poet, painter and sculptor, Lysheha's work is heavily influenced by Chinese literature and philosophy. He has published two collections, *The Great Bridge* (1989) and *To Snow and Fire* (2002). *The Selected Poems of Oleh Lysheha* was translated by US poet James Brasfield in 2000.

KEN BRUEN

Chapter One from *Priest*

'What's wasted
isn't always
the worst
that's left behind'.
K.B.

What I remember most about the mental hospital

The madhouse

The loony bin

The home for the bewildered

is a black man may have saved my life.

In Ireland ? … A black saves your life, I mean how likely is that? Sign of the New Ireland and perhaps, just perhaps, indication of the death of the old Jack Taylor. As I'd been for five months, slumped in a chair, a rug over my knees, staring at the wall. Awaiting my medication, dead but for the formalities.

Gone but to wash me.

The black man leaned over me, tapped my head gently, asked,

'Yo bro, anybody in there?'

I didn't answer, as I hadn't answered for the last months.

He put his hand on my shoulder, whispered,

'Nelson be in Galway this day, mon'.

Mon!

My mouth was dry, always, from the heavy dosage.

I croaked,

'Nelson who?'

He gave me a look, as if I was worse than he'd thought, answered,

'Mandela, mon'.

I struggled to lift my mind from the pit of snakes I knew were waiting, tried,

'Why should … I … give a shit?'

He lifted his T-shirt – it had the Cameroon team on it – and I recoiled, the first stab of reality, a reality I was fleeing. His chest was raw, ugly, with the angry welts of skin grafts. White, yes, white lacerations laced his torso. I gasped, making human contact in spite of myself. He smiled, said,

'They was going to deport me, mon, so I set my own self on fire'.

He reached in his jeans, got out a ten-pack of Blue Silk Cut and a lighter, put a cig between my lips, fired me up, said,

'Now you be smoking too, bro'.

Bro.

That reached in and touched me deeply. Began the process of coming back. He touched my shoulder, went,

'You stay with me, mon, hear?'

I heard.

The tea trolley came and he got two cups, said,

'I put in de heavy sugar, get you cranking, fire your mojo'.

I wrapped my hands round the cup, felt the dull warmth, risked a sip. It was good, sweet but comforting. He was eyeing me closely, asked,

'You coming, bro? You coming on out of there?'

The nicotine was racing in my blood. I asked,

'Why? Why should I?'

A huge smile, his teeth impossibly white against the black skin. He said,

'Mon, you be sitting there, dat a slow burn'.

So it started.

I even went to the hospital library. It was tended by a man in his late sixties, wearing black pants and a black sweatshirt. At first I thought the shirt had a white collar but to my horror saw it was dandruff. He had a clerical air, an expression of gravitas, as if he'd read the manual on librarians and went for the image. It was the one area in the whole place that was quiet, you couldn't hear the quiet anguish so evident in the other rooms.

I thought he was a priest and he stared at me, said,

'You think I'm a priest'.

He had a Dublin accent, which always has that tone of aggression, as if they can't be bothered with culchies (country yokels) and are prepared to battle with any peasant who challenges them. A question to a Dublin person is always interpreted as a challenge. I still wasn't used to speaking. You are silent for months, listening only to white noise, you have to struggle to actually make words. I wasn't intimidated, though, after what I'd endured, I wasn't about to allow some gobshite to bully me. Snapped,

'Hey, I didn't give you a whole lot of thought, fella'.

Let some Galway edge in there. What I wanted to say was, *Jeez, get some anti-dandruff shampoo,* but let it slide. He gave a cackle, like some muted banshee, said,

'I'm a paranoid schizophrenic, but don't worry, I'm taking my meds so you should be reasonably safe'.

The *reasonably* was a word to watch. He looked at his wrist, which was bare, and said,

'Is it that time already? Got to go get my caffeine fix. Don't steal anything – I'll know, I've counted the books twice'.

Stealing a book was truly the last thing on my mind, but if a Dubliner threatens you? The books were a mix of Agatha Christie, Condensed *Reader's Digests*, Sidney Sheldon and three Jackie Collins. A very old volume stood on its lonesome, like a boy who hasn't been selected for the team. I picked it up. Pascal, *Pensées*.

Stole that.

Didn't think I'd ever open it.

I was wrong.

I refused further medication, began to move around, my old limp hurting from the months of inactivity. I felt my eyes retreat from the nine-yard stare, move away from the dead place. After a few days, I was summoned to the psychiatrist's office, a woman in her late fifties named Joan Murray. She was heavily built but able to carry it, her hands were raw boned. A Claddagh ring on her wedding finger, heart turned in. She said,

'You've astounded me, Jack'.

I managed a tight smile, the one you attain when you first don the uniform of the Guards. It has no relation to humour or warmth but is connected to hostility. She leaned back, flexed her fingers, continued,

'We don't see many miracles here. Don't quote me, but this is where miracles die. In all my years, I've never witnessed a restoration like yours. What happened?'

I didn't want to share the truth, afraid if I articulated it, it might revert. Said,

'They told me David Beckham was sold'.

She laughed out loud, said,

'That would do it. I've contacted Ban Garda Ni Iomaire – she brought you here, has stayed in touch about your condition'.

Ni Iomaire. Or Ridge, to use the English form. Daughter of an old friend, we'd been unwilling allies on a number of cases. Our relationship was barbed, angry, confrontational but inexplicably lasting. Like marriage. We fought like trapped rats, always biting and snarling at each other. How to explain the dynamics or disfunction of our alliance? Perhaps her uncle, Brendan Smith, had something to do with it. He'd been my sometimes friend, definite source of information and one-time Guard. His suicide had rocked us both. Against her inclinations, she'd become the source now. I'd helped her look good to her superiors, and maybe my being in her life kept his spirit alive. She was a loner too, isolated by her sexual orientation and on the edge. Lacking others, we clung to each other, not the partnership either of us wanted. Or what the hell, could be we were both so odd, so different that no one else would suffer us.

The doctor asked,

'Do you remember how you got here?'

I shook my head, asked,

'Can I have a cigarette?'

She stood, moved to a cabinet, got a heavy key chain and opened it. You want to know the soundtrack of an asylum, it's the sound of keys. That and a low-toned moaning of the human spirit in meltdown, punctuated with the sighs of the lost. She took out a pack of B 'n' H, got the cellophane off, asked,

'These OK?'

I'd a choice? Said,

'They make you cough'.

And she laughed again. Took her a time to locate matches but she finally got me going, said,

'You're an alcoholic, Jack, and have been here before'.

I didn't answer.

What is there to say? She nodded as if that was affirmation enough, continued,

'But you didn't drink this time. Surprised? According to Garda Ni Iomaire, you'd been sober for some time. After the child's death ...'

I bit down on the filter, froze her words.

After the child's death.

I could see the scene in all its awful clarity. I was supposed to be minding Serena May, the Down Syndrome child of my friends Jeff and Cathy. That child, the only real value in my life. We'd become close; the little girl loved me to read to her. It was a sweltering hot day, I'd opened the window of the second-floor room we were in. I'd been brutalized by a recent case and my focus was all over the place. The child went out the window. Just a tiny cry and she was gone. My mind just shut down after that.

I looked across the desk. She added,

'You were going into pubs, ordering shots of whiskey, pints of Guinness, arranging them neatly and simply staring at the glasses'.

She paused, to let the fact that I hadn't actually drank sink in, then,

'Your Ban Garda brought you here'.

She waited, so I said,

'Fierce waste of drink'.

No laughter, not even a smile. She asked,

'What is the nature of your ... friendship? With her'.

I nearly laughed, wanted to say confron-fucking-tational. But not an easy word to get your tongue round. When I said nothing, she said,

'You're leaving us tomorrow. Garda Ni Iomaire is coming to collect you. Do you feel you're ready to leave?'

Did I?

I stubbed out the cigarette in a brass ashtray. It had a hurler in the centre, the words G.A.A. ANNUAL CONVENTION.

I said, 'I'm ready'.

She gauged me, then,

'I'm going to give you my phone number and a prescription for some mild tranquillizers, to help you through the first few days. Don't underestimate the difficulty of returning to the world'.

'I won't'.

She fiddled with her ring, said,

'You should attend AA'.

'Right'.

'And stay out of pubs'.

'Yes, Ma'am'.

A small smile. She stood, reached out her hand, said,

'Good luck, Jack'.

I took her hand, said,

'Thank you'.

I was at the door when she added,

'I'm a Liverpool supporter'.

I nearly smiled.

That evening, I had my first real meal with the general population. The atmosphere in the canteen was muted, almost religious. Long tables with near a hundred patients gathered. The joys of medication. I got a plate of sausages, mashed spuds and black pudding. I could taste the food, nearly enjoy it, till the TV was turned on. It stood above the room, attached to steel girders, locked down. What? Someone was going to steal it? The opening ceremony of Ireland's hosting of the Special Olympics. A wave of dizziness hit as the face of a special-needs child filled the screen. The reason I was here. Moving back from the table, I stood up. A woman with tangled black hair, nails bitten till blood had come, asked,

'Can I have your grub?'

Palpitations in my chest. A line of sweat coursed down my back, drenching my shirt. Serena May, the only light in an increasingly darkening life.

Dead.

Three years of age and gone because I lost my grip, wasn't paying attention. As I bolted from the refectory, a patient shouted,

'Yo, chow down'.

In my terror, I thought he said, 'Child down'.

Next morning I was packed, ready to leave. My holdall held trousers, one shirt and rosary beads.

The Irish survival kit.

Oh, and Pascal.

I went to find the black man, thank him for his help. I'd a pack of twenty cigs to give him. The doctor had included them with my tranquillizers. The black man was standing in the day room, staring at a newspaper. I mean staring as opposed to reading because the paper was upside-down. I'd learned his name was Solomon, went, 'Solomon'.

No reply.

I hunkered down, tried again. He had slid down along the wall. Slowly, his eyes reached up and he asked, 'I know you?'

'Yes, you pulled me back, remember?'

I offered the cigs and he gave me a petulant look, said, 'Don't smoke, boss'.

I wanted to touch his hand, but he suddenly emitted a piercing scream, then said, 'Fuck off, whitey'.

Later, months on, I rang the hospital to ask if maybe I might visit him, was told his deportation orders came through – the government was deporting eighty non-nationals a day. Using two wet sheets, freshly starched that morning, he hung himself in the laundry.

The new Ireland.

Ken Bruen is from Galway and, after extensive travel, has returned to live in his native city. He has been a finalist for the Barry, Edgar and Macavity awards for crimewriting and was awarded the prestigious Shamus prize in 2003 for *The Guards*, the novel that introduced Jack Taylor to the literary world. *Priest* is published by Bantam Press, 2006.

It was in April 1914 when I first met Rubinstein, that sad, shy man. He came to take part in the great tournament at St Petersburg. It was a glittering, sumptuous occasion, held in the magnificent surroundings of the Yusupov palace. The tournament's distinguished benefactors, whose munificence provided the generous appearance fees and still more generous prizes, included the tsar himself. Thousands paid to attend the games and watch their heroes. I was one of them. I shook the hand of Isidor Gunsberg. I was one of a small group who escorted the venerable Blackburne to Yegorov's Baths, where the Englishman insisted we submit to beating with birch twigs. I was present when the legendary Lasker defeated the rising Cuban star Capablanca, and at the conclusion of that thrilling game I jumped to my feet at one with the crowd to applaud the old world champion's enduring and consummate skill.

And of course I saw Rubinstein. I saw much of Rubinstein. Before the tournament everyone predicted that the Polish genius would carry off the first prize. Even Capablanca, a man not given in any degree to modesty, said in press interviews that he would be satisfied to finish second to the fabled Akiba Rubinstein. Rubinstein's main rivals were either past their prime or not yet fully come into it, whereas Rubinstein himself, then thirty-two years old, was at the height of his powers. He had defeated Lasker in 1909. In 1912 he won at San Sebastian, Bad Pistyan, Breslau, Warsaw and Vilna – five major tournaments in succession! No chess player had ever achieved such a run of spectacular triumphs. There was at that time in his play something of the decisive, organic simplicity of (and I know this will sound preposterous to those who do not love the game, but I stand by my comparison) a Mozart clarinet concerto … or the classical lines of Rossi's best creations, or the streamlined flight of the *Zwergschwan* as it passes over the marshlands on its summer migration to the south. No one could resist Rubinstein. And yet at St Petersburg he failed.

Commentators and historians have advanced many theories to try to explain the mystery of Rubinstein's disastrous performance. And it was a disaster – it is no exaggeration to say it. Had he won, had he even finished second behind the world champion, Dr Lasker would certainly have been forced to play a match against him for the crown. The outcome of such a match, given their respective powers at that time, would not have been in doubt: Rubinstein, born in the remote little village of Stawiski, the youngest of twelve children from an impoverished family, whose father died before he was born and his mother soon after, who spoke only Yiddish and Hebrew until he was almost twenty, would have been the third world chess champion and feted everywhere from Tokyo to Buenos Aires. It was Rubinstein's great opportunity, and he failed to take it. After St Petersburg his chess deteriorated, and since chess was his life, the course of his life could not but be affected by the consequences of the poor moves he made at the board. History passed the great Akiba by. He was to end his days as he had begun them – in poverty and grief – and all because of half a dozen barely perceptibly inferior arrangements of a handful of carved boxwood and ebony pieces on a chequered board of sixty-four squares.

Why did he fail? Some blame J.O. Sossnitsky and the organizing committee for the chaotic conditions in which the early games were played. Such was the level of public interest that the players were virtually walled in by spectators, many of whom were puffing on cigars and cigarettes, and discoursing loudly on the games before them; in Marshall's second-round encounter against Capablanca the crowd was so numerous and unruly that someone pressing in at the table actually knocked over the white king, much to the Cuban's irritation. Such distractions inevitably took a toll on Rubinstein's concentration, but he was not alone in this regard. I can remember to this day how Janowski, desperate for fresh air, rose from the board to fight his way through the throng with all the frenzy of salmon swimming upstream.

Others offer a simple technical explanation: that Rubinstein's opponents had learned from their earlier defeats; they had studied his games, analysed his strengths and discovered his weaknesses, and instead of meeting his pure, logical and unornamented style of play with their usual rococo flourishes and gambits they adapted their own style, tamping it down as the occasion required. Thus Rubinstein found his own weapons turned back on himself, found himself playing against himself, as it were, and was unable to find a way through. As is invariably the case with purely 'technical' solutions, this one is deficient. Capablanca had refined simplicity in chess to an art, he was a past master of the pared down, logical technique that was Rubinstein's hallmark, and yet at St Petersburg he was completely outplayed in the opening by the great Akiba, and managed only by the skin of his teeth to salvage a draw.

Others are nearer the mark when they cite Rubinstein's extreme nervousness and delicate emotional and mental balance. As was already known in 1914, Rubinstein was an unusually reticent man. At our very first meeting he was to confess to me that he believed himself to be odious to others; indeed, he believed his mere presence to be so offensive to his fellow human beings that he sought at every opportunity to separate himself from them. I have had patients exhibiting similar symptoms. Their pathological shyness, when further explored, has often reflected a sense of unworthiness not in themselves but in others; their apparent humility, in other words, served only to mask a profound and sometimes disturbing distaste for their fellow man. This was not – I am confident – the case with Rubinstein, who was gentle and timid. Rubinstein's symptoms had been apparent to his friends for some years, yet they did not stop him winning at San Sebastian, or at Bad Pistyan, or at Warsaw.

The fullest explanation contains a germ of all that has been said above, and yet it is also a great deal more complicated. Chess is rarely the stage for intrigue – if one ignores the gamesmanship of rivals intent on unsettling their opponents, and the interminable bickering over who should or should not have the right to play a match for the world championship; such lamentable and undignified episodes are an intrinsic part of the chess world but are of no interest to anyone other than the enthusiast. But at St Petersburg in the late spring of 1914 there was much more at stake than the mere winning of a tournament, however prestigious. The famous visitors who came to the city to play chess and confined themselves to the luxurious Hôtel de l'Europe and the smart shops and restaurants on Nevsky Prospekt could be forgiven for thinking St Petersburg's founder was exaggerating only a little when he claimed it was 'God's heaven', 'the promised land', 'a sacred place'. The city *is* magnificent (my father was German but I am a Peterburger, born and bred, and proud of my home town). But it is also horribly squalid, and where magnificence and squalor co-exist there will always be rage, cruelty, fear and death. Just as a superficial glance at a chessboard on which a game is in progress will reveal little of the violent struggle under way, so the tourist delighting in the exotic wares on display at the Gostinni Dvor or at the splendour of the Catherine palace will likely be oblivious to the raw, seething currents running through the very streets he tramps in such innocent admiration. Of the eleven players who took part in the great St Petersburg tournament of 1914, only Rubinstein came to understand that death lived in the city, that revolution stalked it. He did not seek this understanding but rather had it thrust upon him. He came to play chess but became embroiled – unwittingly – in conspiracy, betrayal and murder. He never fully recovered from what happened to him, and life subsequently broke him in pieces.

A month before Rubinstein first visited me in my office – he was brought by a mutual acquaintance, the chemist and noted chess amateur P.I. Gorchakov – the body of a young man was recovered from the Neva after a car accident on the Moika Embankment. I read about the tragedy when it happened, which was in the early hours of the morning of March 12th. According to the newspaper, the unfortunate victim was on his way home after a night out with friends and had apparently lost control of his car on an icy stretch of road near the Bear Restaurant and skidded into the river. Such accidents were common enough.

Eight days later, as my secretary was about to go home for the evening, there was a knock at the door. I was waiting for one of my regular patients, whom I shall call Anna V. She was due at seven and I was using the time to catch up on some correspondence. I looked up from my desk to see Mina poke her head around the door. She murmured an apology for the interruption.

I could see at once that something was wrong. 'What's the matter?' I asked.

'There is someone to see you, Doctor', she said.

'Yes?'

'A policeman'. Mina uttered the word in a tone of disapproval. 'He insists he see you now'.

I frowned and got up and went to the door. In the small outer office where Mina worked was a pale, slightly built man of about thirty-five. He held his hat before him and his dark hair was lank and greasy with an unkempt fringe that fell in front of his eyes. These were blue, a blue so light it appeared unnatural. His upper lip was thin, almost non-existent, but the lower was full, indeed fat; it was practically an anachronism on a being who was otherwise so entirely spare and bloodless. I'm afraid I probably stared at it.

'Dr Spethmann?' he said. His voice was thin, high and nasal; it was not a pleasant sound.

'Yes', I answered him, somewhat warily.

'I am Inspector Lychev. I wonder if I might speak with you privately'.

I was, naturally, already curious. It was the first time a policeman had been to my office and I couldn't help a fleeting sensation of excitement enter my heart: the work of a psychoanalyst is not unlike that of a detective; both involve bringing to the surface what is being withheld or hidden, and for a moment I imagined myself being called on to assist in some important investigation. 'Of course', I said. I turned from that fat lower lip to Mina, who already had her coat on. 'Go home, Mina. I shall see you in the morning'.

'Are you sure, Doctor?' she asked solicitously; evidently, she had not formed a good impression of the policeman and appeared unwilling to leave us alone.

'Yes, yes', I reassured her.

She hesitated for a moment, then nodded. 'Goodnight, Doctor', she said, before skirting round the policeman in an attempt to put as much space as possible between them. She pulled the outer door to very gently after her.

'Please', I said to Lychev, showing him into my office.

I went behind my desk and he sat in the old armchair at the head of the couch, though it meant he had to twist a little to face me. He took in his surroundings quickly and expertly. I saw his gaze linger over the Incan and Moche artefacts arranged in spaces between the books lining my shelves; everything was being weighed and assessed for clues about their owner.

'How may I help you, Inspector?' I asked, pleasantly enough.

'You can start by telling me how you came to know Alexander Yastrebov'.

I did not care for his tone, and it was my irritation at his brusqueness that caused me to delay my reply. He seemed to think the hesitation suspicious. His pale eyes narrowed and before I could say anything he asked querulously, 'Does the question discomfit you?'

'Not at all', I said; I had no idea who this Yastrebov was, and since I knew myself to be innocent of any crime I should have been confident in relation to the policeman, especially one so slight and unprepossessing. But in truth I felt uneasy. We all live with guilt, of course, we all have secrets, so it is hardly surprising that the unexpected arrival of a policeman should have provoked mild anxiety in me. 'I'm afraid I cannot help you', I said, evenly enough. 'I do not know any … Yastrebov'.

Lychev said nothing. He ran a finger across his forehead to clear his fringe, then patted the hair at the back of his head; the movement was oddly feminine. He sucked in a deep breath, then let it out slowly, a sigh that seemed to say:

'Here we go again. They always start out by denying it. It would save so much time and be easier for all of us if for once they would just admit what they have done'.

He reached slowly into his overcoat. 'Yastrebov was a student', he said at last.

I shrugged.

'You're certain you don't know him?'

'Certain, yes'.

'Then how do you explain this?' Lychev said. Withdrawing his hand from his inside pocket he produced a plain, unused envelope and passed it across the desk. 'Look inside', he said.

I did as he commanded, and removed a water-damaged business card. The ink was smeared but the wording still legible.

'Do you recognize it?'

'Of course I recognize it', I said. 'It's my card'.

'Can you explain why Yastrebov was in possession of your card?'

'He could have come by it in any number of ways', I explained. 'I give my card to my patients, of course, but also to associates, acquaintances, people I meet at scientific conferences or at receptions and dinners. They sometimes pass them on others. I'm sure I don't know half of those who end up with my card'.

'Could you have given the card directly to Yastrebov?'

'If I did it was without knowing who he was', I said. 'Who is he anyway? Does he say I knew him?'

Lychev looked at me carefully in frank assessment of my honesty; he made no pretence otherwise. 'Yastrebov is dead', he said; then he added, with no more drama or emotion than if he were recalling the weather last Tuesday: 'He was murdered'.

I waited for him to continue. Instead he got to his feet. 'Your office is very pleasant', he said, looking about.

I hardly knew what to say. He moved to the chess table I keep to the side of the window and lifted a white knight, which he scrutinized, then tested its weight. 'A nice set', he said. 'English?'

'Yes', I said.

'It's a good design, more pure. Do you play?'

'When I can, which is not often', I answered him. 'How was Yastrebov murdered?'

Lychev replaced the knight and looked up at me. 'He was drowned – deliberately drowned – then placed in a motorcar which was pushed into the river. It happened near the Bear Restaurant'.

'But of course!' I exclaimed. 'I read about this. But there was nothing in the paper about it being murder'.

'The murderers attempted to conceal the crime by passing it off as an accident'.

'Why?'

'Why did they try to pass it off as an accident?'

'Why was he murdered?'

'I have my theories, but we shall see', he said; he did not seem eager to expand; and he added phlegmatically as he moved to the door: 'Everything always comes out in the wash – in the end'.

'I'm sorry I couldn't be of more help', I said.

Lychev smiled for the first time, and for no obvious reason. His top lip curled upwards at the sides to reveal inflamed gums and small, discoloured teeth. 'I will see you tomorrow afternoon at police headquarters', he announced abruptly. 'Be there at five'.

Again, the peremptoriness took me by surprise, as much as the nature of his command.

'What?' I objected.

'I would advise you to be punctual'.

'I've told you – I know nothing about any Yastrebov'.

'Perhaps we will discover that you can be of more help than you think'.

'I have an appointment at five – a patient'.

'Would you prefer to come with me now?'

I did not answer; this was getting more ridiculous – and unsettling – by the moment.

Lychev looked at me squarely. 'So, five o'clock tomorrow'.

'Very well', I said, anxiety and annoyance growing in me at equal rates.

I saw Lychev to the outer door. I was trying to think of who I might call to have the matter cleared up. Then he said, 'You have a daughter?' I flinched visibly at this. 'Catherine, no?'

The thought of this odious man knowing – merely *being aware* – of Catherine's existence was enough to strike terror into my heart. 'Yes', I said coldly.

'Bring her with you tomorrow'.

I do not think I uttered a single word for a minute or more; I simply stared uncomprehendingly at my unwelcome visitor. Even when the shock subsided still I did not speak. I did not ask why he wanted Catherine to come, or what on earth he thought Catherine had to do with Yastrebov, or this business of the accident or murder or whatever it was. I knew there would be no point, so I said nothing, not even to bid him goodnight.

Lychev swept his lank fringe out of his eyes, carefully patted his hair and put on his hat. 'I will see you tomorrow, Doctor Spethmann', he said.

And with that he was gone from the office. Unfortunately, it was a lot longer before he was gone from my life.

Ronan Bennett was born in Belfast in 1956. He is the author of four novels: *The Second Prison* (1991); *Overthrown by Strangers* (1992); *The Catastrophist* (1998); and *Havoc, In Its Third Year* (2004), which was nominated for the Booker Prize. His latest novel, *Zugzwang*, is currently being serialised in *The Observer* and will be published by Bloomsbury in August.

Hugo Kelly

In Townsville

The visit to the Rowes Bay Residential Care Centre did not start well for Joseph. On the way the air conditioning stopped working in his car and he slowly cooked in the industrial heat and humidity of the midday sun. Then Townsville with its quaint English names confused him. Kensington and Hyde Park and Buckingham Street blended into a series of identical roads and avenues that he drove up and down for almost an hour searching for the home's reception. Eventually when he was about to give up he chanced upon the red-bricked main building with its flat roof and marked parking spaces. Inside the pale light coloured everything in sepia and the few residents he saw moved in a different gravity, pacing up the tiled corridors in slow, deliberate steps. There was the sound of weeping that gradually ebbed into silence. Afternoon radio then filled the air, a synthetic DJ talking about crazy holiday traffic. In the background he realised the weeping had started again.

At the reception a pretty blonde nurse smiled at him and he felt self-conscious. Large damp patches had appeared down the front and back of his T-Shirt and his thinning hair was stuck to his head. Dignity was hard to muster. Here I am his presence stated: a sweating Irish man, a refugee of air conditioned environments.

'I'm looking for Frank Joyce,' he said.

The smile cooled to politeness.

'Ah Frank,' she said. 'He's a character isn't he?'

She directed him out into an area surrounded on one side by motel like rooms and on the other by a row of thin, dusty trees. The heat hung over the day like a poultice. Joseph found Frank sitting outside the door of his room. A television blared from inside. He was older than Joseph had imagined. A line of spittle ran from the corner of his mouth and his Irish skin hung like white loaf bread from his thighs. His dull eyes affirmed that he was nearly blind as Joseph had been told.

Joseph coughed before speaking.

'Hello Frank. I'm Joseph – Jim Kelly's nephew – I rang you earlier.'

Frank shifted a fraction in seat, then scowled.

'Where the hell were you? I've been waiting all morning.'

'I'm sorry,' Joseph mumbled, 'I got lost finding the place.'

'Dinner's coming up soon,' Frank said in a sulky voice.

A woman in the room next door peered out nervously. Her body was tiny, squeezed by age and her pale skin looked painted onto her skull so that every bone and ridge was apparent. She touched her upper lip nervously.

'Mr. Joyce would you please turn down the television?'

'Piss off Erna,' Frank roared back.

Erna retreated into her room again.

Joseph sighed. He had exchanged his Saturday with Tanya, for this glimpse of melancholy. It was she though who had told him to come in the end.

'You've been moaning about it for a week. Just get it over with,' she said.

He had laughed, enjoyed her pleasing frankness. In many ways she represented Australia to him; a brash health and beauty that could be strange and yet at times absurdly familiar. In truth he knew little about her. She had been married before. Once she had mentioned a name in her sleep. Steve. He had lain there in the air conditioned chill wondering who Steve was. Her former husband? An old lover? In the morning he had decided not to ask her. It was enough for him that they got on with the day to day business of living. That seemed a good Australian sentiment to him as well.

'How do you find the home here?' Joseph asked.

'The Aussies are a crowd of thieves.' Frank snarled before flapping at an imaginary insect that was bothering him. Joseph looked away into the perfect blue of the sky. The man was far more confused that he had realised when he had agreed to the visit. Hard to reconcile him with the person he had once seen in an old photo with his Uncle Jim. The two men looked tough and strong and handsome in that nineteen fifties way. Behind them the Snowy Water Dam was taking shape, the great engineering project that was the stuff of legends and outback romance. Afterwards his Uncle had returned home but Frank had drifted following casual jobs and his luck. It was the classic tale. Life lived in the permanent present of the emigrant, old age the only punctuation.

'What's the dole at home?' Frank growled.

Joseph scratched his head.

'Ah. It's around a hundred and fifty euro,' Joseph said.

'Heh?'

'About a hundred, hundred and twenty pounds I suppose in the old money'.

'A hundred and twenty pounds.'

'Frank's face lit to one of complete wonder.

'A hundred and twenty pounds!'

He slapped his pale thigh with delight and giggled to himself.

'I think the old age pension would be about hundred and fifty pounds,' Joseph added.

At this Frank appeared completely confounded.

'No,' he said. 'It couldn't be.'

'It is,' he insisted. 'That's what it is now.'

'Oh Jesus … oh Jesussssssss.'

The head bowed again, only lifting to whisper.

'A hundred and fifty pounds. A hundred and fifty pounds. There weren't two jingles on a tombstone when I left the place.'

A trail of ants was moving along the concrete path. A couple had entangled themselves in the curled white hair of Frank's leg. Joseph felt he should brush them them off but he was afraid of this intimacy.

'When was the last time you were home?' he asked.

Frank appeared not to hear him.

'Did you ever jump from the mill?'

Joseph frowned, tired of this scattered conversation. He glanced at his watch. If he left now his Saturday afternoon might be saved.

'Do you mean Mangan's Mill? On the quay at home?' he said.

'What other f-ing mill is there?'

'You used to jump from the mill?' Joseph repeated.

Frank smiled for the first time.

'I was the only one to ever jump.'

It was difficult to imagine such a thing. The building stood like a tired sentry, marked by rust and decay at the disused quay. Joseph had once explored it, listening to the sound of mice and rats scattering as he approached. From the roof he had nervously looked down. The sea, a sour green colour had rumbled and shunted like an animal in pain.

'It must be a two hundred foot drop,' Joseph said with admiration.

There was no response. Frank was motionless again. His face was covered in a new, darker emotion. He moaned suddenly like a young child might do and Joseph wondered was he ill. He jerked forward and grabbed Joseph's wrist.

'There's something I want to tell you,' he said. 'I did something bad. I did something very bad.'

His grip tightened.

'I left someone when I shouldn't have. I left her when she needed me.'

His eyes grew thick with tears and his head lulled from side to side, murmuring as he did so. There was such sadness that Joseph was shocked but it was also unstable, tainted with anger, self-hatred perhaps.

'I'm haunted,' Frank mumbled.

'It's ok,' said Joseph, 'it was a long time ago.'

'I miss home,' Frank blubbered through his grief. 'I miss it. But I can never go back.'

Joseph felt a heaviness descend, draping across his shoulders so that the lightness of Australia seemed diminished. This is not what he had expected at all. Frank was now crying to himself in long heaving jolts. Joseph knelt down on one knee in front of him so he was looking directly into his trembling face. He wondered what he should say. For once it was easier to tell the truth then make up some bland comment.

'You're not alone,' Joseph said, 'I've done something bad as well.'

His voice faltered. Frank momentarily became still.

'I'm seeing someone,' he said. 'My wife is back in Ireland. It's this woman Tanya I met at the University where I'm lecturing ...'

He words grew tangled but he mumbled on.

'It's not that serious. They say adultery is ninety per cent opportunity ...'

He looked up at Frank's blank expression. He had no idea whether he was being understood at all. It was ridiculous. So very ridiculous. But still he stayed kneeling like he was for a minute, perhaps longer. He noticed that the ants had climbed Frank's leg as far as his knee. Gently he brushed them off onto the ground where they scattered along the bright concrete into the grass.

There was a shuffle of movement. Joseph looked up and saw that Erna was staring at him from the door of her room.

At that moment a silver haired nurse appeared across the yard.

'Dinner Erna, Frank,' she called out.

This seemed to rouse Frank.

'Lamb chops today,' he said with anticipation.

He staggered to his feet and stretched out a trembling hand to Joseph.

'It was nice meeting you. Someone from home.'

'Yes. Yes. I'll visit again,' Joseph said. 'I'll take you out. Perhaps we could go for a bite to eat or maybe to the sea if you would like that.'

He thought Frank was listening but then the man's eyelids flickered shut and a wide smile beamed across his unshaven face.

'One hundred and fifty pounds' he said with great pride. 'One hundred and fifty pounds'.

The Nurse approached Frank and took his arm. Erna now emerged from her room. She stared at Frank in deep suspicion and then said to the Nurse,

'That man there is having an affair with another woman. My Bill would never have done that.'

The Nurse offered a surprised smile, glancing at Joseph with amusement.

'Now Erna,' she said, 'I think you need a good dinner.'

Frank was oblivious. Already he seemed to have forgotten everything that had happened, the five minutes of opera and pantomime that had occurred.

Joseph stood in the shade of the trees and watched the three of them until they turned the corner and disappeared from view. He walked back towards his car, remembering with despair the broken air conditioning.

The heat inside was almost overpowering. He opened all the windows though it did little good and sweat poured down his brow onto his face, stinging his eyes. He tried to remain calm, wanting to think clearly for a moment. All that would come to mind though was Frank. He saw him as a young man leaving the town land at home. Who had he left behind? Some poor girl who had been pregnant? Perhaps it had just been love and he had run from fear of that. And then he saw Frank younger again, on top of the old mill sprinting towards the edge of the building. Then the childish body all angles like a kite hurling through the air, drifting from an arc to the sudden fall. The explosion in the water and the few faltering seconds before the wet head appeared in the sea, all bright-eyed with a wide misleading smile. The rippling Atlantic flicked the bright seeds of sunlight around him. Everything, anything must have seemed possible. So little he thought is really experienced after the age of thirteen.

He started the car, sliding the automatic car into reverse. As he did so he glanced in the mirror back towards the home and half imagined he could see Frank there, standing looking after him. They were both alike he mused, two men trying to deal with the outcomes of decisions taken and not taken. He hoped that the man might find some peace after today though he had no idea whether that would be the case.

He drove off accelerating quickly. The sudden speed he hoped would bring relief from the clawing heat.

Hugo Kelly has been writing short stories for a number of years. His work has appeared in the *Sunday Tribune*, the 1999 and 2005 Fish Short Story Anthologies, and *Books Ireland* amongst others. He was twice shortlisted for a Hennessy Award for Emerging Fiction and a children's story has recently been broadcast on RTE Radio 1. He has won a number of awards including the 2006 Maria Edgeworth Award and the 2005 UK Children's Writers and Artists Story Competition.

ADRIAN FRAZIER

'Where does spirit live?' Houses in Modern Irish Literature[1]

1

In May 2002 I was going into Kenny's bookshop in Galway, and Art O'Sullivan was coming out of it. Art lives in Carnacun where Moorehall is located. While teaching in the local school he established a George Moore weekend, held annually in the summer or autumn to honour winners of writing contests for young and old, in fiction and poetry. Like many little literary festivals around the country it is a most pleasant occasion. Less successful has been Art's scheme to persuade county and national authorities to pay for the reconstruction of Moorehall, a ruin since it was burned out by the IRA in early 1923, at the fag end of the Civil War. Art was halfway home to Moorehall's restoration, with the land donated and part of the money promised, when Government surpluses turned in a blink of the eye into Government deficits, so Moorehall is a ruin still, in spite of the best efforts of one of the best of men.

This started me thinking about a question Seamus Heaney poses in the sequence of poems called 'Squarings' (1991):

> Where does spirit live?

In its context, Heaney's question has to do with poems, and with life after death, and even more, in that sequence, with houses. What do the things-we-live-in have to do with the things-that-live-in-us? Are some buildings better habitudes for the life of the spirit than other buildings? Can you enrich a person's being by housing that person among beautiful pictures, in light and space and comfort, surrounded by bountiful gardens, familiar furniture, with storied carpets, magical suntraps, portraits of ancestors looking down from high walls, places in a hallway and closet nooks with special associations from time past?

Or look at it the other way: can you spiritually deprive somebody by housing them inside poor architecture, and walling them up with luxurious consumer goods specially selected for their ugliness?

W. H. Auden famously thought so, and spoke of certain domestic habitations in the city and out in the country as doctors, healers of what ails us:

> Publish each healer that in the city lives
> Or country houses at the end of drives.
> Harrow the house of the dead; look shining at
> New styles of architecture, a change of heart.
>
> – 'Petition'

To start off with Moorehall in particular, what might those walls on that hill above Lough Carra, beside that ruined garden enclosure, in front of a broken down stableyard, mean to anyone, now that all that lived there are dead? Put aside for a moment Art O'Sullivan's notion that it could serve as a revitalizing centre for a local community, a magnet for tourism, and source of recreational activities – horseback riding, trout-fishing, reading in leisurely rooms about local history ... fine eating too, I hope. That's all *sensible*, and the government, when it had money, sometimes must have spent it on worse things. But I am not talking about the sensible and utilitarian value of houses; instead, I am talking about another value than either auction price or use-value, if there are any other such values.

One can see that Moorehall and its contents meant something to George Moore himself, because he tells us so. That meaning had nothing utilitarian about it, because the house and grounds remained important to him in spite of the fact that for sixty years he chose not to live there, and rarely visited. In February 1923, during the Irish Civil War, George Moore, then of Ebury Street, London, had no inkling that Moore Hall had been used with his brother Maurice's permission to quarter Free State troops. In GM's imagination, up until 1 February 1923, Moore Hall lay quietly on the hill above Lough Carra, slowly decaying into a ruin like Castlecarra, Castlebourke, and the little pile on Castle Island, now all quiet around the lake. There is no evidence that George Moore ever did learn why Moore Hall was burnt.

Writing to Richard Best eight months later, Moore said he did not think he would ever be able to visit Ireland again: 'The burning of my house forbids; I should crumble into dust the moment I set foot on the shore'.[2] His mind began to turn once again away from the present toward a dreamy tale of lovers in Castlecarra, a time long ago before guns, automobiles, nationalism and sectarianism, when all that was ruined was in its first flush, Ireland was covered in great forests, people traveled only by horses or on foot, and storytellers were abroad in the land. Yet three years would pass before Moore could turn this dream into a book, his fifty-first, *Ulick and Soracha*.

For the time being, in order to complete *Conversations in Ebury Street*, Moore wrote a poetic elegy for the Moores of Moore Hall inspired by a portrait of his grandfather, the historian George Moore. When GM was a boy of eight, his parents took down another beloved portrait of his grandfather, an early one painted when he was a boy in green Spanish court dress, and compared GM with his grandfather, point by point. As he grew up, GM wanted to be like his clever grandfather who wrote books, the sixty-year old man in the golden frame, in 'the prim chocolate-coloured coat, one shoulder showing against the dead gold of the armchair, and the voluminous cravat swathing him chin-high'.[3] Over the decades, GM found himself 'becoming the portrait of my grandfather in old age' – 'the high, round forehead, the large nose, the small, truthful eyes':

> For my eyes are truthful, I said to myself; they belie me if they are not; and I fell to thinking that though truthful they did not tell a soul as beautiful as my grandfather's. He brought, I said, a beautiful soul into the world and took it away with him, leaving little of it to his son, and none, I am afraid, to his grandson. But I regret nothing, for had Nature given me my grandfather's beautiful soul – a soul of almost Virgilian melancholy – I should have remained at Moore Hall, reliving my grandfather's life.

It was better, GM judged, that he had left Ireland for cities where he was more at home, Paris or London, and used Moore Hall only as a 'dreaming house': 'his spirit going forth at the end of the day's work to wander in the deserted corridors, in and out of the empty rooms, the doors opening before him, everywhere meeting pleasant detentions, finding one in an almost forgotten water-colour, another in a faded curtain of remembered pattern, and still another in a chess-board ...'

> [M]y dreaming house is gone, with only the portrait saved to hang on the first landing in Ebury Street in a little lobby, whence it looks out and catches my eyes as I come downstairs, a sort of fetch-light or corpse-candle, reminding me that my race is over, betrayed, scattered, and in exile. Every race has its day, it says, and every creed; every grief, every joy, dies sooner or later. Memory outlives the dead; it, too, dies, but we are powerless to crush or bury it; and were I to remove the portrait to a garret and turn its face to the wall, my grandfather's eyes would still haunt and oblige me to rehang it in the lobby, for I shall lack strength always to write to the director of a public gallery and ask him to relieve me of it.

2

It would presumably be rich to recall a childhood spent in a house with a great library, a stable of racehorses out the back, old watercolours by family members to be found lying on a desk, next to a chessboard that had been there since you were born. But it is not necessary to indulge in the sort of laughable and off-putting nostalgia for what never in fact was, shown by that Shakespeare scholar, A. L. Rowse, born to a working class family, a fact he regretted, who used his Oxford fellowship to pal up to titled English folk, then wrote in his diary when he stayed for a weekend in a big house, that he always thought he was the sort of person who should have been born in a house like that, rather than, as he brutally put it, in 'the [fuck]-hutches of the millions'. Not just great houses become dreaming houses.

At the end of a day, your mind too probably wanders in the deserted rooms of the home in which you grew up. In those rooms, every object is like a poem or a picture, in that the things symbolize more than they say or show on the surface, much more; they are numinous. Spirit, to answer Seamus Heaney's question, lives in them.

This kind of picture-memory of a place is crucial to being a person. Maybe it is crucial to being a duck or a sheep, we don't know. Without an interior architectural order of images, often borrowed from one particular house, the inner lives of humans might not have the same degree of volume, continuity, and unity. Out of what looks like a purely random accumulation of personal properties, postcards chosen by whim from otherwise forgotten vacations, snapshots of no photographic value, things that 'ought to be thrown out' but are not because for so long they haven't been, out of such a medley of things, a collection of symbols is built up that represents a home. These symbolic images indicate the floorplan of an half-imaginary, half-real home that stretches out inside of us. It is a home in which a certain people dwelt and it then dwells in different ways in each of those people, and also in those across the road or down the hill.

Moorehall, for instance, was not just a dreaming house for the Moores, but for those down the hill as well. When I was interviewing people in Carnacun for my biography, quite a number could describe in vivid detail the place before it was burnt, and the ways of the community as they were structured by the presence of the house. Usually, this was not from their own memories, but those of their parents, who evidently talked of the days gone by again and again. As they too remembered those memories, the children, now old men and women, were fond, or bitter, or remorseful, or just dreamy, as people are when they recall family members no longer alive. The house itself, though they never entered it, was as psychically significant as a person central to their own life-stories.

3

The ancients believe that that memory and houses are connected, and further that by understanding this connection, one could enlarge one's mental power. This art of memory was discovered by a Greek poet named Simonides (556 BC-c 468 BC). The circumstances in which he made the discovery are, strangely enough, like those in which a vacant Moorehall, even after its burning, became George Moore's dreaming house.

It happened this way. Simonides was at a banquet given by a nobleman in Thessaly and attended by many lords and their families. The nobleman offered Simonides ten gold pieces for a praise poem. So the Greek lyricist composed and sang a poem in honour of the nobleman, but also giving praise to the twin gods Castor and Pollux. The nobleman then paid Simonidies not ten gold pieces, but five, and told him to collect the rest from Castor and Pollux. A little later, a message was brought in to Simonides that two young men were waiting outside who wished to see him. He rose from the banquet and went outside, but there was no one there. Just then the roof of the banqueting hall fell in, crushing the nobleman and his family, and his guests and their families. The corpses were so mangled that the relatives who came to take them away for burial were unable to identify them. But Simonides remembered each one of the guests, and pointed out where they had been sitting, so the bodies were claimed by the kin.

When asked how he could identify so many strangers, Simonides realised that it was because he associated them with the places at the banqueting table at which he had first seen their faces. Orderly arrangement of things to be remembered within a house appeared to be ideal for memory. He concluded that a person wanting to increase the power of memory should construct a mental picture of a house and symbolic images of the things to be remembered, which would be stored in a certain place within that house. The order of places would preserve the order of things, and the images of things would denote the things themselves. This theatre of symbols, he suggested, would be like a wax writing-tablet and the letters written on it.[4] The art of memory founded by Simonides was practiced by the great minds of Europe from the 5th century BC until the 16th century.

4

Houses, symbolic images, and memories may all be important to a powerful and orderly imagination, but the house does not have to be a big house; that's certain. Seamus Heaney has written a great number of his poems, often the best of those poems, about a Derry cottage beside a railroad track, where he was born, and about a borrowed slate-roofed Wicklow cottage where he spent a few years with his own children. Consider one poem about the clay floor of a cottage in Derry[5] (number 40, from 'Squarings'):

I was four but I turned four hundred maybe
Encountering the ancient dampish feel
Of a clay floor. Maybe four thousand even.
Anyhow, there it was. Milk poured for cats
In a rank puddle-place, splash-darkened mould
Around the terracotta water-crock.
Ground of being. Body's deep obedience
To all its shifting tenses. A half-door
Opening directly into starlight.
Out of that earth house I inherited
A stack of singular, cold memory-weights
To load me, hand and foot, in the scale of things.

Those 'memory-weights' are the symbolic images which Simonides says we should store in a mental theatre, to order our minds, so we can know our minds. Heaney's terms are both precise and suggestive: the actual house – its feel and apertures and shapes – is for the self a ground, a measuring scale, an opening into starlight; it connects us with the lives that came before us in that place, so that, while being four, we possess the memory of one who was four hundred or four thousand.

I like also the double-sided image of inherited property, as something that loads one down, almost ties one up 'hand and foot', but at the same time gives one a sense of justice and proportion, like a set of weights and scales. The same double-sidedness of a certain kind of property, family property let's call it, is united in the latin word 'impedimenta', which means the baggage one would take if moving from one place to another, things so precious that, even though they were heavy and bulky, and one had to travel by horse, one would still have to bring them all along, so that these things would turn out to be also, not just one's valuables, but one's impediments, always underfoot and in the way. There is the same difference between this sort of family property and consumer goods themselves as between a house and a home: one is the bearer of symbolic power to awake a deep inner life, and the other is not.

In the case of Heaney's poem, a mud-floored cabin has the same power as Coole Park, the now destroyed home of Lady Gregory, celebrated by Yeats for its:

> Beloved books that famous hands have bound,
> Old marble-heads, old pictures everywhere;
> Great rooms where travelled men and children found
> Content or joy ...
>
> ... ancestral trees
> Or gardens rich in memory glorified
> Marriages, alliances and families,
> And every bride's ambition satisfied.

Great trees, books, pictures, themselves monuments of the spirit, may indeed be good things, but it is not only the rich whose gardens may be rich in memory glorified. The poet here is just a little bit too much like A.L. Rowse waking up in the guest room of a big house, and thinking, Now this is just the house in which I *should* have been born. Still, Yeats may be right when he goes on to say that greatness and glory will be lost if we sell up and shift about as 'fashion or mere fantasy decrees'. What would Yeats have said had he lived when the estate agent was king, and gazzumping had replaced gazebos?

In another poem from *Squarings*, number xxxiii, Heaney himself questions the value of a certain kind of new house. Whether it is the newness of the house or its design, he finds the house hard to praise, although it is a house his father designed:

'Plain, big, straight, ordinary, you know,'
A paradigm of rigour and correction.
Rebuke to fanciness and shrine to limit,
Stood firmer than ever for its own idea
Like a printed X-ray for the X-rayed body.

This house of correction sounds like prison. But it also sounds like many new block-built, plain, big, ordinary bungalows, which in fact is what it was. It is a description of the house in the town of Bellaghy where Heaney's father moved his family from the Derry cottage – setting for so many of the poems – when the poet was fifteen years old. It represented a changeover from the charm of backwardness to unpicturesque, unmagical modernization with all the mod-cons and two dormer windows. 'Like a printed X-ray for the X-rayed body'. Not the real thing.

Drive out the road from Galway towards Spiddal, or Oughterard, or Headford, or Tuam, and observe the new bungalows unrolling like a ribbon alongside the route to Ballinrobe. Each one faces the road, set back a regulation fifty metres on a bulldozed site, with no features of the earlier topography or vegetation. Each has a port for the car, just as the 19th century long house had a byre for the cow or the pig. The ones built since the 1980s often have a front portico of faux-Spanish arches, dormer windows, and a patchwork anthology of building materials: pebble dash, whitewash cement, stone-cladding, wood-siding, brick of many colours, pillars of reconstituted granite, lintels of reconstituted sandstone, and quoins in alternating light and dark stone. There is an evil book called *Bungalow Bliss* by a Meath architect. It is reissued in a new edition every year, and every year it is sold out. Inside is a catalogue of the possible features of an Irish bungalow, and those who hire a builder to put up a house in a farmer's fields (farms are simply present or future building sites) can mix and match features selected from the pages of *Bungalow Bliss*.

5

The fear of losing both one's soul and one's tribal memory also shows up in the witty couplets of Vona Groarke's 'Open House', which is not about bungalows but a brand-new housing development of semi-detached residences.

> At first glance every house looks much the same
> as the others adjoining and sharing the name
> of Sycamore Court (though there's barely a tree
> to be seen and there's certainly no royalty).
> instead we have seventy-six ideal homes
> laid out with the stature of so many tombs
> in severe straight lines that all run parallel
> concluding in debris that doesn't bode well
> for the 'intimate setting' or 'rural surrounds'
> suggestive to buyers of huge estate grounds.

By the end of the poem, a woman in one house lives the same life as the man in the next, so, it is concluded, they might as well live together as an ideal couple, like other seventy-five ideal identically ideal couples in the estate. This is a housing scheme for producing the identitiless population of *Brave New World*.

Clearly, however, for a house to have meaning, it need not be a home in which many generations of a single family were born and died. In the title poem of *Other People's Houses*, Vona Groarke revisits one of the houses she rented with her husband before they were married. The place is 'not looking good./ There['d] been a fire and the roof's caved in'. She wanders through its rooms, and remembers the radio, the mattress, the couch – no old marble-heads, no old pictures anywhere, but still symbolically significant of their young love, when they lived in other people's houses. Now they've 'a stake in a place of [their] own'. She then remembers and repeats the promise of lasting love between them, in a wonderful echo of the last lines of *Paradise Lost*:[6]

> I want you to know, not that nothing
> is lost – even I could not promise
> so much – but that something remains,
> here, even after so many years:
> the starlings are still nesting in the eaves.
> And last night as I watched them
> their circular orbit put me in mind
> of the rhumba you danced with a bumble-bee
> right there at the gate, on the day that we left
> this house behind us, together and for good.

The final poem on dreaming houses that I want to consider is by Medbh McGuckian, the Belfast poet. It is called 'Marconi's Cottage', but it isn't about Guglielmo Marconi, the Italian physicist with an Irish mother who invented radio teleography in 1896, though it does concern a seaside cottage on the north coast of the island, once owned by Marconi, and later acquired by McGuckian herself. It may also be about something else – one can never be absolutely sure about a poem, especially one by this poet. Much of McGuckian's work from this period concerns her recently dead father. In certain ways the poem speaks of Marconi's cottage as the poet would speak of her father.

For instance, the house like her father is all that she has 'gathered of otherness'. Just as with certain houses we live not just inside them, but they also come to live within us, so a male, a complete Other, such as a father – usually outside or even opposed – can live within his daughter, and happily so.

In the poem the worn glisten of the flesh of the house brings to mind the worn body of the poet's father, 'relearned and reloved'.

She wants to keep the house 'for what we call forever, the deeper opposite of a picture', as time and three-dimensionality are vaster than a spatial image and two-dimensions, as the never-in-this-life-apprehended afterlife may be less ephemeral than the life it follows.

Maybe the house is like a god, as McGuckian says; certainly it is haunted, and not by Marconi, but by the poet's imagination.

6

Those who compare religions say that a belief in the spirits of the dead, especially of ancestors, is an early form of belief out of which many institutional religions grew, religions which then turned around and condemned the belief in ghosts as popular superstitions. Yet a belief in ghosts is more credible than much that is taught in theology. Of types of ghost, one of the most attractive is the ghost that belongs to a house; it becomes, as we say, a haunted house. This country was a home for many who believed in ghosts and haunted houses. What kind of house is it that gets haunted? Deserted houses, almost always, or those occupied by a few last members of a once large family; houses big or small where forbidden love was enjoyed, and cannot be forgotten by the dead lovers, or where unspeakable crimes of passion are relived by tormented souls, killing again or again being killed. Or houses vacated by whole villages in time of famine, that then become associated with pain and dread. The number of haunted houses seems a result, then, of famine, poverty, pain, and mass emigration: first of the tenantry, then of the landlords.

None of this is cosy, or at all like home, but it is yet one more testament to the attachment of something in humans – usually called the spirit – to particular habitations, where the memory of intense experience is so powerful it outlives the body that underwent the experience. It demonstrates immortality by means of spine-tingling.

One does not much worried about modern civilization being bothered by ghosts as being deserted altogether by memory, beauty, and being in one place for good. It is not that life is spiritually richer in a grand house like Moorehall, or in a cottage in a village by the sea, or in county Derry when farmers ploughed with horses rather than tractors. The distinction between city and country is here not relevant. Paris doesn't seem spiritually empty, and everyone believes the bridges over the Seine have been consecrated by stolen kisses. Nor is the glory of fine architecture, as one finds in Paris, a necessary condition for spirit taking up shelter within. Families may begin – many do, I believe – on a flea-market sofa in a suburban bed-sit, and the pattern on that sofa may become the memory palace of the children who first learn to stand holding onto its cushions.

But one does worry over the destruction of old houses and the putting up of rowhouses never meant to last, never meant to be loved, never meant to do anything but meet the minimum standards of a planning board and make money for a developer. 'Where does spirit live?' Not there, surely not there. Wouldn't that mean that where so many young couples have no choice but to live in such houses, no others being built in numbers, and the population growing fast, that there will be more humans but less spirit? No, it cannot mean that! That would be too depressing. Humans often rebel against circumstances inadequate to their wishes, and out of imagination create beauty to spite the ugliness their eyes behold. The culture of letters has been so richly glorious in Ireland over the last three decades, inventive of forms of poetry, drama, and fiction that are vernacular, Catholic (or post-Catholic), and modernist, it is a pity that its material culture – while ever so much more cash-rich than in the past – is so low-minded. It is reasonable to think that all such tracts of tenements as have been built in the last twenty years will be torn down in another half-century. They're not built to last anyway; and such have always been torn down again and again. Then we'll see what comes next – maybe some dreaming houses.

Notes

1 Talk given at the Erris Literary Festival, Co. Mayo, 27-29 June 2003

2 GM to Best; 17 October 1923; Harry Ransom Humanities Research Center.

3 *Conversations in Ebury Street* (1924), 289.

4 Frances Yates, *The Art of Memory* (Chicago: University of Chicago Press, 1966), 1-2 (quote is from Cicero, De oratore). Heaney's 'Squarings,' xix, concerns this art of memory (*Opened Ground*, 345).

5 It may be that the cottage in this poem is not Heaney's home place, but another in the area. If it were his own, why would the poet be four years old when he first encountered the damp feel of its floor?

6 Vona Groarke, *Other People's Houses*, 53.

Adrian Frazier is Director of the MA in Drama and Theatre Studies and the MA in Writing at NUI, Galway. He has published on Irish poetry, drama, and fiction of the 20th century, including the monographs *George Moore 1852-1933* (Yale, 2000) and *Yeats, Horniman, and the Struggle for the Abbey Theatre* (Berkeley, 1990). He is currently working on the 'Hollywood Irish': Abbey Actors in Hollywood, 1936-1953.

Acknowledgements

Thank yous to:

Maura Kennedy for all her help in the compilation of this anthology.

Tomás Hardiman for his enthusiastic support of the new publishing and distribution initiatives for the *Cúirt Annual* in partnership with Arlen House.

Maeve Curtis for administrative support.

Pauline Bewick for permission to reproduce her 2005 watercolour, 'Kissing her Book'.

ColourBooks, Dublin for sponsorship of this publication.

Adrienne Foran, ColourBooks.

Ireland Literature Exchange for their support of the translations of the work of Maram al-Massri and Abdelwahab Meddeb.

Máire Holmes, facilitator of Galway Arts Centre's creative writing courses.

Ray McDonnell, designer of the Cúirt brochure.

Sincere thanks to all the authors and translators.